Save Montessori
from
Social Justice

SAVE MONTESSORI

FROM
SOCIAL JUSTICE

Woke Montessori Schools are Betraying
the Teachings of Maria Montessori

By Charlotte Cushman

Copyright © 2025 by Charlotte Cushman

All Rights Reserved

Cover design by Mary Aly

Book layout by Mark Van Horne

ISBN: 979-8-9918852-0-1

This book is dedicated to Carol Landkamer,
my best friend, who said to me,

"It's the few individuals who make the difference."

"...it is the psychology of the child, the life of his soul, that has gradually dictated what might be called a pedagogy and a method of education. If I can be said to have a method of education, it is one based on the psychic development of the normal child."

—MARIA MONTESSORI
Education and Peace

Table of Contents

Introduction ix

Chapter 1 Education
    The Purpose of Education.. 1
    The Process of Thinking.. 5
    Authentic Montessori Education 11

Chapter 2 Social Justice
    Progressive Education 25
    What is Social Justice? 29
    Marxism 33
    Paulo Freire... 36
    Queer Theory 38
    Drag Queens 43
    Gender Transition 52
    Furries 56
    Fake Pronouns 58
    Pedophilia 59
    Restorative Justice.. 61
    Revisionist History 67
    The Family.. 68

Chapter 3 Montessori Organizations That Promote Social Justice
    Association Montessori International (AMI).............. 73
    American Montessori Society (AMS) 84
    National Center for Montessori in the Public Sector (NCMPS) 98
    Montessori for Social Justice (MSJ) 98

Chapter 4 Conclusion
    Stand Firm.. 105
    Save Montessori... 108

Appendix A The Tale of the Pilgrims 113
Appendix B Save Western Civilization—
Defend Christopher Columbus 117
Appendix C The Unknown Story of Pocahontas 121

Bibliography 125

About the Author... 147

Introduction

Unfortunately, some Montessori organizations have caved to the social justice movement.[1] Two major Montessori organizations, Association Montessori International/USA (AMI/USA)[2] and the American Montessori Society (AMS),[3] have supported or sponsored conferences that featured workshops or lectures on understanding structural racism, diversity, anti-bias, LGBTQ students, and much more. These conferences were put on by an organization called Montessori for Social Justice.[4] The website for the AMI/USA conference in 2018 states that Montessori for Social Justice is, "... dedicated to promoting anti-bias, anti-racist Montessori education. They bring together Montessorians of all trainings to work towards educational equity and the success of all children."[5] Another Montessori organization, the Montessori Foundation, formed a task force to address and act on several issues such as eradicating prejudices, establishing a social justice curriculum, and so on.[6]

In 2020, I was accepted to speak on child discipline at a conference at the Montessori Education Center of the Rockies (MECR), but they cancelled my appearance when they learned I disagree with implementing so-called social justice in Montessori. They did not express any concern about my talk. Instead, they cancelled me because they disagreed with my views. Here is the letter I received:

> We haven't met, yet I have a heartfelt message to share about MECR's stance on Social Justice. The pandemic delayed the planning and execution of the upcoming Montessori in the Mountains conference for two years. Back in 2020, you were accepted as a presenter. It has come to our attention that in the interim, you wrote an article for American Thinker

---

1. However, not every Montessori school or teacher supports the social justice movement. If you are considering sending your child to a Montessori school, investigate their position on it carefully.
2. AMI/USA, "Montessori for Social Justice Conference," *AMI/USA* 2018.
3. David Ayer, "Montessori For Social Justice," 2016.
4. Montessori for Social Justice, *Montessori for Social Justice*.
5. AMI/USA, "Montessori for Social Justice Conference," *AMI/USA*, May 7, 2018.
6. Kathy Leitch, "Standing Together," *The Montessori Foundation*, June 30, 2020.

in June 2021, "Is Social Justice Posturing on Track to Contaminate Montessori Education." AMS and AMI have been promoting a necessary evolution in the views of the Montessori community concerning Social Justice. MECR fully supports this worthy work.

Here is where we stand. Historically, we acknowledge that Montessori has not been accessible to the global majority and want to be a force for change in this area. Over the past two years, we have been offering Diversity, Equity, and Inclusion (DEI) training for all instructors, and we plan to expand that training every year. We have asked all instructors to integrate DEI principles into their content area. We also plan to do DEI work with our students at all levels. MECR has also been consciously working on diversity in hiring new instructors and invitations to new Board members. This work is just the beginning of our journey, and we know there is so much more work to do. With bold humility, we will diligently and conscientiously work towards a more equitable and just balance where we follow ALL of the world's children.

Because of our conflicting messages, we can no longer offer you a speaker position at this event. We have removed your presentation from the program and apologize for any inconvenience. You are welcome to attend the conference to join in community with other Montessorians.

Here is my letter to them in response:

It is clear that I was discriminated against for disagreeing with the social justice movement. Diversity, real diversity, is tolerating people with different opinions. What happened to "equity?" Why don't I qualify to be treated fairly? Or does equity only apply to those with privilege on the Left? Discriminating against people who disagree with you is an outrage, especially coming from an educator/representative of an educational philosophy that teaches independent thinking.

If you are interested, here are my reasons for opposing the social justice movement. Social justice is grounded in Marxism. It is the theory that society is divided into two classes, the oppressed and the oppressors. Social justice seeks to take from the oppressors and give to the oppressed. This is done by preaching that a certain group is inherently racist and evil so that a bias is created against them. It is an ideology that places groups higher than individuals, and holds that all groups should be equal. If there are any disparities in group outcomes, it is attributed to discrimination and group injustice rather than individual choices and

Introduction

actions, and therefore the more successful groups need to be punished. This results in groups constantly fighting for power over each other.

To say that a person is inherently racist because of the group he belongs to (i.e. skin color) is determinism—the view that a person has no free will, and therefore has no choice in how he thinks or acts. Determinism is the antithesis of Montessori's view of human nature: *"Free choice is one of the highest of all mental processes."*[7] Social justice does not belong in Montessori.

I am disappointed that you do not recognize that Montessori has the antidote to racism and it has always had it—free will and individualism. Instead, you have turned Montessori into a tool for politics. Montessori is not politics; it is an educational approach for every individual child. It is universal for every child. Social justice, the idea that people are determined by their group or other circumstances, rather than their individual minds, will destroy Montessori.

Conferences should be a means to inspire people to think for themselves, rather than telling them what to think. Presenting your attendees with only one side to the controversy of social justice is brainwashing. It is dishonest because the unspoken message is "This is the only way to view this topic." In order to foster independent thought, and in order to make the conference fun and exciting, the conference needs to be open to other sides. This would foster much discussion and lively debate, leaving people with differing viewpoints with something to think about, and come to conclusions based on that thinking.

Disagreements are healthy and they are needed for a culture to flourish. There is no moving forward without them. Listening to only one side of a controversy is stagnating, and frankly boring. Bringing new ideas into the mix is stimulating, and necessary for creativity and human advancement.

Even though I was not going to speak about social justice, the fact that you have removed me from speaking shows that you are censoring [suppressing] me because of the fear of a different point of view. Yet if your view is right, there is no reason to be afraid. The social justice warriors are trying to squelch free speech. Freedom of speech is one of the founding principles of this country, and trying to kill it for disagreements is wrong, and even worse than that, it is evil. If you want to know why

---

7. Maria Montessori, *The Absorbent Mind*, (Dell) 271.

our country is currently divided, it is precisely because of the problem of treating those of us who disagree as lesser humans.

You did not name one thing that was false in my article in the American Thinker. Not one. That is because there wasn't anything. It takes courage to stand against what one knows to be wrong. I have that courage. Your choice to censor me will not stop me. And I will not apologize for working to help save our freedom of speech, nor will I apologize for my opinions.[8]

My conflict with the Montessori Education Center of the Rockies was the catalyst for my mission to save Montessori from devastation. Social justice will not only contaminate Montessori education, it will destroy it. Social justice needs to be exposed for what it is—a dreadful ideology with the ultimate goal of destroying capitalism and freedom. Parents who have enrolled their children in Montessori deserve to know that Montessori organizations are turning political. While not every Montessori school is implementing social justice, it is the trend.

To understand a movement, such as social justice, one needs to understand its Marxist history and the activists who are driving it. There are some people who think that social justice is just a way to be kind to each other. That isn't what it's about at all. At root it's about power and control.

This book explains what the child needs for his survival and happiness, how the Montessori Method provides it, and how social justice sabotages it.[9] Chapter 1 lays the foundation of understanding the child's needs as Maria Montessori explained them. Chapter 2 defines social justice, its background, elaborates why it's terribly harmful, and explains what happened in education that enabled it to thrive. Chapter 3 names four Montessori organizations and some accredited schools and presents information about their positions on social justice presented at Montessori conferences, at webinars, on websites, and in articles. (Please note, these are not the only Montessori organizations pushing social justice, just the most prominent.) I talk about restorative justice, the transgender movement, the truth about drag queen story hour, furries, pedophilia,

---

8. Charlotte Cushman, "Montessori Teacher Fights 'Social Justice'," *American Thinker*, March 12, 2022.

9. This book does not completely explain the Montessori method. For a more comprehensive explanation, see my first book, *Montessori: Why It Matters for Your Child's Success and Happiness*.

Introduction

revisionist history, and the family, and describe the effects they have on children and Montessori education as a whole.

So as not to reinvent the wheel, I have included some of my articles that were published in the online publications, *American Thinker* and *Capitalism Magazine*. Some of them were altered a little for clarity or to avoid repetitions.

For clarity and emphasis, I have italicized the quotes by Montessori.

I owe a great deal of gratitude to people who read my initial drafts of this book and gave me their reactions, helpful comments, and advice. Many thanks to my husband, Dan Van Bogart, Carol Landkamer, Emily C., Ronald Pisaturo, Sunny Lohmann, Carla Sheldon, and Andrew Bernstein. I am grateful to Robert Sharp for editing the book, Susan Sheridan for proofreading the book, and Mark Van Horne for formatting it.

I do not support social justice, wokeism, and so on, and have been called intolerant and racist because of it. So be it. First, I never consented to be tolerant of immorality. Why am I supposed to be tolerant of people who push social justice, but they don't have to be tolerant of my dissenting views? Second, people who do not have a rational argument direct smears and insults to those with whom they disagree. It is a common tactic to silence dissent. I will not be silenced.

My goal for this book is to alert parents of this infiltration so that they can be careful not to enroll their children in a Montessori school that has been contaminated with Marxist ideology. I also want to see Montessori organizations reject social justice and all ideologies that are contrary to the Montessori Method.

One of my biggest frustrations throughout the years has been the Montessorians who, time after time, cave in to every educational fad that comes along instead of consistently applying the Montessori Method they claim to represent. I hope this book gives them the courage to go against current trends.

CHAPTER 1
Education

The Purpose of Education

We live in turbulent times. Our culture has been on the decline for a long time and it is getting worse. Drugs, violence, and inappropriate sex seem to dominate what we read in books and see on the screen, not to mention what is actually being done in the real world. The death of George Floyd during the summer of 2020 sparked rioting, looting, property destruction, defunding of the police, and the burning of our cities. This is not how civilized people resolve conflicts. Can Western Civilization survive?

While American cities were being burned down, the rioters were shielded. The police were told to stand down.[1] When citizens took measures to protect themselves against the rioters, they got in trouble,[2] while the rioters were set free.[3] Nothing was said about the devastation caused by the rioters, but when someone fought back against them, there were roars of indignation. Voting by mail was advocated to prevent the spread of COVID, but it was just fine for hundreds of rioters to assemble closely together as they caused mayhem in the streets. A CNN reporter even called the riots in Kenosha, WI, "mostly peaceful" as buildings were burning in the background.[4]

Our country, our lives, and our homes are under attack. Organized groups such as Black Lives Matter, Antifa, Marxists, Environmentalists, and the World Health Organization have openly voiced their support for human extinction and abolition of the United States.[5] Criminals commit

---

1. CBS News, "Minneapolis police precinct," *CBS News*, May 29, 2020.
2. "St. Louis couple facing charges," *Baltimore Sun*, August 25, 2020.
3. RT News,"Catch and release," *USA News*, June 3, 2020.
4. Khaleda Rahman, "CNN Mocked," *Newsweek*, August 27, 2020.
5. Paul Taylor, *A Respect for Nature*, 115. In this book he stated that the "total, absolute, and final disappearance" of human beings would enhance the wellbeing of the earth, and be greeted with a hearty "Good riddance!"
David Graber, "Mother Nature as a Hothouse Flower," *Los Angeles Times*, October 22,

violent crimes such as theft, murder, and assaults and are soon released from jail only to commit the same, or worse, crimes again.[6] The FBI is sent to intimidate political opponents by arresting peaceful protestors, raiding their homes, and seizing their personal property.[7] Felons were let out of jail early because of the coronavirus ostensibly to save their lives, then some went on to take the lives of others.[8]

Tolerance, which is touted as a virtue of the political Left, goes right out the window when dealing with those with whom the Left disagrees. The expression, "Innocent until proven guilty," seems to have little meaning. The world pronounced Kyle Rittenhouse and Derek Chauvin guilty before the evidence was in and certainly before the trial.

Children are being treated solely as objects of sexual desire. In other words, they are being sexualized. They have been exposed to, and have even participated in, drag queen shows where men, who are dressed as over-sexualized women, degrade women and the sex act, while adults cheer it on. This degradation of sex is also done in public schools with the use of pornographic books and drag queen story hour. Parents, who are paying the taxes for their child's public education, are called terrorists when they protest this horror.[9] Pedophilia is being defended by claiming it is an unchangeable sexual orientation and should be accepted by society.[10]

1989. In this article, he openly expressed support for human extinction when he wished for "the right virus to come along."

Bill Gates, "Bill Gates – Population – Vaccines," *YouTube,* December 9, 2010. He stated that we could lower population if we do a "really great job on new vaccines, health care, reproductive services."

Patricia Cullors, "BLM Co-Founder Patrisse Cullors," *YouTube,* June 19, 2020.

Lilith Sinclair (@LaughAtLibs), "Black Lives Matter leader," *X.com,* July 17, 2020. She admitted that she was organizing for the abolition of the United States.

6. "Woman savagely beaten in NYC…," *ABC News,* September 28, 2022.

7. "FBI charges multiple individuals," *Live Action,* October 5, 2022.

Jack Davis, "Shortly After Targeting Conservative Media," *Western Journal,* November 21, 2021.

NextNewsNetwork, "BREAKING: FBI Seizes Personal Property," *rumble* (video), August 10, 2022.

8. Todd Betzold, "Convicted murderer released from prison," *Front Page Detectives,* November 18, 2021.

"Inmate released early, arrested weeks later for murder," *Law Enforcement Today.*

9. Sam Fenny, "Texas AG Urges Prosecution," *David Icke,* October 21, 2022.

Tyler Durden, "Texas AG Urges Prosecution," *Zero Hedge,* October 19, 2022.

10. Emily Jones, "Scholar Calls Pedophilia," *CBN,* July 21, 2018.

Freedom of speech has been threatened. The government pressured social media platforms to silence opposing political opinions.[11] The movement of political correctness sprang up in various forms throughout history in totalitarian regimes for governments to control their citizens. And now it is entrenched in the United States. Good ideas are vital to a thriving and growing culture, but our youth can't handle ideas, that is, they can't handle the ideas that they have been told are bad ones. College students have become so upset about hearing controversial ideas that some have committed violence on college campuses, and people have defended this violence.

Our economy is in danger from the national debt and the devaluing of the dollar. Our national debt could bankrupt the country, which means all of our personal saving accounts would be emptied or made worthless. There is danger of a complete collapse.

Politically, we are at a crossroads between capitalism and socialism, between freedom and subservience. Socialized medicine, laws restricting free speech, mandated vaccinations, government takeover of private property, and so on are real threats. There are parallels between what is happening in the U.S. and other countries that are already socialistic. Arguments between friends and family are rampant because we are in a war, not a kinetic one, but a philosophical one.

The chaos that we see in the world today is because there is something that adults were not taught when they were children, and had they been taught it, we wouldn't be going through these turbulent times. So, as parents and educators, what do we need to teach children so that no matter what the future holds, they will be able to handle it? What is the purpose of education? This is the fundamental question, and the wrong answer means our children will not be equipped to stop the end of Western Civilization.

In nature, animals have certain characteristics which are essential for their existence. Some animals can run very fast in order to catch their prey. Eagles have sharp eyes so that they can find food. Some animals change color to protect them from their enemies. But what do we have? What can humans do that is essential for their survival, but that is different from all the other animals?

---

11. Rachel Bavard, "Government dictating what social-media bans is tyrannical," *New York Post*, July 16, 2021.

The answer is how to *think*—the process of identifying and integrating the facts of reality.

> *... reason in the final analysis is what distinguishes a man from irrational beings. A man is one who can make a reasoned judgment and then, through an act of the will, decide his own course of action.*[12]

This is the central purpose of Montessori education—both to impart an essential set of facts and to teach and train children to think rationally and clearly so we best equip them to live in the real world and thrive.

To underline the point, thinking is crucial to human life itself because thinking is our means of survival. We humans have no instincts for survival. If you were to go into a forest, would you automatically know which berries were poisonous? Which mushrooms you could eat? No. Everything we know about survival has to be learned; we have no spontaneous survival mechanism. By the same principle, we do not know automatically which system leads to flourishing and which leads to starvation—capitalism or socialism. So, the choice to think or not is the choice to live or not.

Not only can man's mind observe which berries make one sick, it is his mind that can use logic (the non-contradictory identification of the facts of reality) to figure out which doctors are competent and which schools are good. Man can even discover medical cures and launch rockets into space, and he can do all this because his mind is unique in the animal world—it can reason. It is reason that man needs in order to survive and live happily, but a child has to learn how to think and thinking takes effort. This is why a proper education is critical.

If a child knows how to think, he[13] can figure things out on his own and seek his own answers based on the facts of reality. A person who thinks can rely on his own mind and therefore feels confident. We all know people in school who got straight A's because they had what people call a photographic memory—this is not thinking. These same people, remember, could not answer an essay question. Thinking is not memorization or regurgitation of memorized procedures. A thinker can relate one

---

12. Maria Montessori, *The Secret of Childhood*, (Ballantine) 96–97.

13. To avoid confusion, I generally refer to the child as "he" and teachers as "she" except when I cite a specific incident where the child is female or the teacher is male.

thing to another, can solve problems, and can visualize consequences. He grasps the facts of reality and can deal with them long range. Thinking is not easy, thinking is work. It is also fun.

The Process of Thinking

I will now explain how one develops knowledge—how true thinking is done, first on a basic level, and then on an increasingly abstract level—and then show how concepts and ideas are formed in a child's mind from the sensory inputs he gets directly from reality. In the next section, you will see how Montessori education in particular encourages this process in children. It is technical, so bear with me because I think it is important to understand what the child needs to learn in order to think and why a proper education matters.

Everything that man perceives about reality must first come to him through his senses, but these sensory inputs do not constitute knowledge. The brain must interpret, integrate, and conceptualize these sensations before they become knowledge. Man's senses tell him *that* it is, but not *what* it is. What it is must be learned. Humans and animals are alike in that they receive perceptions (sensations automatically perceived by the brain), but man is unique from all other creatures because he can take the next step—he can conceptualize. (Perceptions are automatic, conceptualizing is not.) A concept is a mental integration of two or more concretes which are different but share essential characteristics and are the same by definition. In other words, we isolate the essentials or similarities in things and then integrate them into a concept.

For example, take the concept "tree." First, we observe the concretes. We note similarities and differences between trees and keep the underlying essentials in our minds. The essential attributes of trees are leaves, branches, trunk, and roots. Once the concept is formed, we give it a name, "tree." After forming the concept "tree," we don't have to start over again on the perceptual level and examine all the differences and similarities of trees. We can instantaneously identify a tree because the concept tree includes certain essentials that are consistent with all trees. Children must learn to form concepts, first simple ones, then more complex. The Montessori materials are specially designed to teach children how to do this.

Language and math are involved in forming concepts: math in figuring out relationships and language when a word is assigned to the concept in the last step of the integration. In forming the concept of tree, we know it has leaves, but no particular size leaves and no particular number of leaves. Trees have trunks, but no particular height or width.

In the process of conceptualizing, man learns attributes which are aspects of an object which can be separated conceptually, but not separated from the actual entity, such as color, length, width, rough, smooth, and so on. This process is called abstraction.

Knowledge has a hierarchy. The child starts out at the perceptual level and begins at the beginning with what is called first-level concepts. Then he works on second-level concepts, but he has to know the first-level ones to grasp the next level of concepts. Some higher-level concepts can be widenings, some can be narrowings. A first-level concept would be 'chair.' A wider second-level is 'furniture' or a narrower second-level concept is 'rocking chair.' Another example of a first-level concept is 'dog,' second-level wider is 'animal' or narrower 'collie.' Another first-level concept is 'tree' and second-level concepts are 'forest' or 'oak.'

As the child gets older, he forms higher concepts by adding more and more information to his earlier concepts. He learns that the leaves of deciduous trees are green, but they turn color in the fall; coniferous trees have green needles and some turn brown in the fall. He learns the names for different kinds of leaves and the parts of a leaf, the kinds of roots, how a tree grows, what it needs to live, the process of photosynthesis, and so on.

As the child moves forward to learn higher abstractions, any new information must be consistent with what he has learned before. This is an important point. Contradictions in the facts of reality don't exist. Any apparent contradictions left uncorrected confuse the mind and sabotage the child's ability to understand reality, which undercuts his self-confidence. Confusions must be resolved for the child to develop a competent, integrated mind.

Concepts must be developed sequentially and logically. You cannot learn calculus before arithmetic, and you cannot learn how to diagram a sentence before you know how to read. You cannot learn about photosynthesis until you know what a plant is. Conceptualization cannot be developed haphazardly. Each level builds on the ones below it.

Because we humans can conceptualize and reason, we can think beyond the immediate range of the moment and can create airplanes, chart maps, go to the moon, cure diseases, etc. What is critical to know is that understanding does not happen automatically. At the perceptual level, memorization is the child's mode of functioning, but as he gets older this needs to change. Instead of learning through memorization, he needs to learn through reason. If he doesn't understand what he learns, he will memorize it, won't retain it in many cases, and will develop a poor memory.

The primary purpose of education is to help him learn how to reason, so that he can live a good life as an adult. Knowing how to reason will result in self-confidence and happiness. Education must bring the child above the concrete, perceptual level to that of effective conceptualization. The educator must guide the child step by step toward developing a reasoning mind, a mind that can draw abstractions from the concretes of reality. A reasoning mind constantly shifts back and forth from the concrete to the abstract and back again. This is how the mind functions.

If the mind doesn't operate correctly, the person remains concrete bound and can't form principles. Suppose you tell a child, "Don't throw rocks at cars. If you do, it could break some windows and damage the car. It could also cause an accident and people could get hurt." So, he stops throwing rocks, but the next thing you know he is throwing sticks at cars. When reprimanded, he replies, "Well, you didn't say anything about sticks." He has violated the principle of "throwing things at cars is dangerous." Another result of a mind that doesn't operate correctly is the person who becomes a rationalist. The rationalist forms conclusions or principles, but they are not grounded in reality. The rationalist pays no attention to facts on the ground; he goes right to his conclusion and then tries to find facts to support it. To use the example of the principle above, let's say the driver of a car is terrorizing a pedestrian, and our subject has a chance to stop him by throwing a big rock at the car, but the man won't throw the rock because "throwing rocks at cars is dangerous." Principles must be grounded in reality and the thinking mind knows how to do this. Context matters.

> *Man is guilty of a like sin against the intelligence when he employs his creative activity of thought for its own sake, without basing it upon truth; by so doing he creates an unreal world, full of error, and destroys the possibility of creating in reality.*[14]

---

14. Maria Montessori, *Spontaneous Activity in Education*, (Robert Bentley) 242.

Here is an example of the process of thinking with higher-level concepts, concepts that adults are concerned with like... "turbulent times." Suppose someone tries to determine if our government is acting appropriately.

- To decide this, he needs to understand the philosophical branch of politics and the role of government in men's lives. Do citizens have rights? If so, what are they? Should the government use force against its citizens? Should the government restrict free speech? Should the government enforce voluntary contracts between individuals? Should the government control the monetary system? Should the economy be regulated? Should the government regulate business? Should a government be limited in power? What are the principles of a proper social system?
- However, to answer these questions, he needs to understand and answer the questions that come before it in the philosophical branch of ethics that address the nature of man. What *is* the nature of man? Does man need values in order to survive? Why? What are those values? How does one determine what are the right ones? Is man an individual? Is man basically good, bad or born *tabula rasa* (blank slate)? Does man have free will or is he determined by forces beyond his control? How should men interact with each other—trade or theft? Is the initiation of the use of force against others moral? In order to live, does man need freedom? What are the requirements for man's survival?
- However, before he answers questions about ethics, he has to understand the philosophical branch of epistemology, or the study of knowledge. What do you know and how do you know it? Is knowledge automatic? Does man acquire knowledge through a process of reason or from repeating what he has heard? Is reason enough to comprehend reality? Can man make mistakes? How does man know when his conclusions are valid? Can man be certain of anything or is he doomed to live in a state of self-doubt?
- The answers to these questions rely on the philosophical branch of metaphysics, or the study of reality. Is reality chaos? Or is it knowable? Is there only one reality or is it different for everyone? Is what you see real or an illusion? Can you change reality?

Can you see from this how the correct development of higher-level concepts relies on the proper development of the concepts that come before them in sequential layers, each layer relying on the foundation that came before it as well as constantly referring back to reality? Every decision a person makes, from whom he votes for to what school he sends his child to, is based on concepts, which are based on earlier concepts, which eventually come back to his fundamental understandings about reality.

Concrete bound people and rationalists have a disconnect between facts and principles. They go through life having a hard time following a train of thought from one to another and can't make connections between ideas. Since they are so confused and find thinking so difficult, they rely on what they hear others say and just go around repeating what they have heard. Montessori thought that one should not accept something as truth without evidence:

> *Credulity is, indeed, a characteristic of immature minds which lack experience and knowledge of realities, and are as yet devoid of that intelligence which distinguishes the true from the false, the beautiful from ugly, the possible from the impossible.*[15]

She thought that credulity, accepting something without evidence, was the characteristic of an uncivilized man:

> *… credulity may exist in adults; but it exists in contrast with intelligence, and is neither its foundation nor its fruit. It is in periods of intellectual darkness that credulity germinates; and we are proud to have outlived these epochs. We speak of credulity as a mark of the uncivilized.*[16]

People who don't know how to think operate on their emotions instead. Now there is nothing wrong with emotions, but emotions are not thinking. They are responses to what a person values based either on his own independent thinking or on what he has been told to think. People who operate on their emotions have a hard time recognizing contradictions, thinking about them, and resolving them. They can't follow a line of logic. People who are emotionally triggered can't think. If a person has a negative reaction to a prospective employee because of his skin color, he needs to introspect. He needs to ask himself why he feels negative. When

---

15. Maria Montessori, *Spontaneous Activity in Education*, (Robert Bentley) 259.
16. Ibid.

and why did he come to the conclusion that skin color mattered? Is his conclusion true? How does he know it is true? Or is it false? The person who operates on emotion does not introspect to correct his misconceptions about reality. He feels it so it must be true.

However, the thinking person is able to dig into the facts. When he does, he realizes that skin color does not determine a person's character and this realization should cause him to change his mind. Reason is a reverence for facts and a fully honest commitment to organize our understanding of the facts logically. In every single case, we must look at the facts first, regardless of our feelings. We must cultivate a reverence for facts and truth in our children.

Persistent contradictions and illogicalities do not bother people who don't know how to think. Many don't even recognize inconsistencies because they actively evade contradictions. Some even think that contradictions are normal. They do not operate the same way as rational people. They have "narratives" that they defend, and manipulate or even invent their own "facts" to fit those narratives. Therefore, they twist, ignore and even make up facts with no compunction. The result is mental difficulties, confusion, and eventually mental illness.

> *Just as vice, which is an exercise of function without purpose, wastes the body until it becomes diseased, so imagination unsustained by truth consumes the intelligence until it assumes characteristics akin to the mental characteristics of the insane.*[17]

If you want to know the reason for this disrespect for facts, consider what is taught in most colleges, especially in philosophy classes. Students are told that there is no such thing as reality, and that reality is different for everyone. They are taught to disregard facts or, even worse, that they don't exist.

Ideas matter. And false ideas that are accepted have negative results. If there is no such thing as reality, a violent riot can be called peaceful, and insults and smears can be called tolerance. Since facts don't matter, why wait for all the evidence before pronouncing someone guilty? Why let due process take place? Why have any official discourse? Why not just destroy cities instead?

Those who think reality is unknowable, live in a state of confusion. If

---

17. Maria Montessori, *Spontaneous Activity in Education*, (Robert Bentley) 266.

a person does not operate by identifying the facts of reality, or even denies that reality exists, the only other way to function is with emotions and whims. As you watch the videos of rioters threatening, pushing, yelling at citizens or police, laughing or clapping when a policeman or someone with opposing views is hurt, giving people the finger along with all their colorful language, notice their emotions. Take note of the look of hatred on their faces and ask yourself if these are people who know how to reason. Do you think they are capable of sitting down and having a civilized discussion to determine facts and solutions?

If a child is not taught how to think, his development is stagnated and he remains at the perceptual and emotional level of functioning. Just like these rioters.

Authentic Montessori Education

Montessori recognized that the ability to reason was unique to humans.

> *A child starts with nothing and develops his reason, the specific characteristic of man.*[18]

She invented a system that meets the requirements for developing the child's capacity for rational thought. The Montessori Method teaches children how to think by instituting the four requirements of reasoning ability: knowledge of reality, an orderly mind, exercising one's will, and intellectual independence. I'll address each of these in turn.

Knowledge of Reality. To think successfully, humans need to know what exists, and what exists has to be learned because the baby is born without any innate knowledge. Reality is the starting point in the pursuit of knowledge. Knowledge is always knowledge of reality.

> *... in order to develop the imagination, it is necessary for everyone first of all to put himself in contact with reality.*[19]

> *The mind that works by itself, independently of truth, works in a void.*[20]

---

18. Maria Montessori, *The Secret of Childhood*, (Ballantine) 61.
19. Maria Montessori, *Spontaneous Activity in Education*, (Robert Bentley) 250.
20. Maria Montessori, *Spontaneous Activity in Education*, (Robert Bentley) 242–243.

The baby leaves the monotonous womb and comes into a world with sounds, lights, textures, colors, temperatures, and so on. What are they? Notice how infants pursue knowledge without any urging. They reach out to touch objects and put them in their mouth.

> *The senses, being explorers of the world, open the way to knowledge.*[21]

They watch us intently and eventually learn to crawl, walk, and talk without any formal lessons from teachers or parents. Infants exhibit an enormous amount of concentration and joy in their learning. Children have a normal and natural desire to learn.

As the child works on the sensory impressions he has received, he develops his reasoning ability:

> *A child develops through personal effort and engagement... It is of utmost importance that a child be able to recall the impressions he has received and be able to keep them clear and distinct, since the ego builds up its intelligence through the strength of the sense impressions which it has received. It is through this hidden inner labor that a child's reason is developed.*[22]

The baby's mode of learning continues beyond infancy. The child needs to be gathering perceptual data in much the same way he did when he was an infant and moves away from the need to observe and touch <u>very gradually</u>, but without reality as the starting point, intelligence will not grow.

> *The power to imagine always exists, whether or not it has a solid basis on which to rest and materials with which to build; but when it does not elaborate from reality and truth, instead of raising a divine structure it forms encrustations which compress the intelligence and prevent the light from penetrating thereto.*[23]

The child eventually needs to be able to visualize what he has learned so that he can think about it. As adults we can consider alternatives in our heads, we can picture this possibility and that possibility, but the child

---
21. Maria Montessori, *The Absorbent Mind*, (Dell) 183.
22. Maria Montessori, *The Secret of Childhood*, (Ballantine) 96–97.
23. Maria Montessori, *Spontaneous Activity in Education*, (Robert Bentley) 265–266.

can't do that at first. He needs to physically move objects around to consider options. The Montessori child begins to learn how to consider alternatives when he sorts objects according to color, shape, texture, size, and so on. The fact that young children cannot visualize explains why when you ask a young child what happened, he turns around and looks back at the location of the incident. Visualization is something the child has to learn and is based upon his experience with the real world. The child initially learns concepts by touching and manipulating actual objects rather than merely looking at pictures of those objects (which is more abstract and comes later). The classroom is full of hands-on materials. A few examples are the geometric shapes, size distinction activities, practical life activities, and math and language materials. Montessori also helps the child to visualize with color coding activities. One can see that in the counting chains where the quantity of one is red, two is green, three is pink, and so on. After working with those beads, the child eventually begins to visualize those beads and add them in his head.

The child's understanding of reality is unstable so he tests it. Children are learning about reality for the first time and don't know what will happen, what is real and what isn't real. Babies will drop a spoon from their high chair over and over and then watch to see what happens. Will it fall each and every time? When I was a child, I stuck my finger in an outlet more than once to see if I would get shocked again. At age five, I grabbed the steering wheel as my dad was driving to see his reaction. And I did it a second time to see if he would react the same way.

Here are some comments and questions from children, ages two to six, in my classroom that illustrate their perceptions of reality:

- The children wanted to know if reality is what they perceive it to be. "If you show me, then I've been shown, right?" "One, two, three, four, five, six, seven. Is this seven?" "One, two, three, four. Do I have four?" "What are you doing?"
- They wanted to know what exists. "What's that noise?" "Is there such a thing as monsters?"
- They wanted to know if reality can change. "Where is daddy?" Ten minutes later, "Where is daddy?" Ten minutes later, "Where is daddy?"
- Since young children have no idea of time and can't see consequences or think long range, they live in the immediate range of the moment. "When will I be a baby again?" "Is today now?"

- They also have no concept of cause and effect. "I didn't break it. It was an accident."
- Children would become very upset because they didn't understand that just because someone says something, it doesn't make it true. "That child said I don't have a brother, and I do! Do I?" "He said I'm mean. Am I?"
- Some children would think that if they said something enough, it would make it so. They thought reality could be changed by lying. "I didn't do it Miss Char." "I didn't do it." "I didn't do it."
- Children have very real fears based on their rudimentary understanding of reality. Even upper elementary children can be frightened by certain movies, TV shows, etc. Because of those fears, I sometimes heard statements such as, "I'm afraid that witch will come out of that book and get me."
- "Have you ever been a purse?" This was asked by Joey, a four-year-old child. While this question is unusual, it illustrates the enormous amount of information that the child needs to sort out. Facts of reality that are so obvious to adults are not self-evident to the child.

Notice that young children are figuring out the first philosophical level, metaphysics. They are asking the first questions about reality. Are they in a universe that is knowable? Or is it an incomprehensible chaos? Does reality keep changing, or does it stay the same? Are the things they see real—or are they an illusion? If someone says something, does that make it true? Can they or someone else change reality?

The child wants to learn about the real world and has a difficult time distinguishing the difference between reality and fantasy, especially up to the age of six. Blending the two can be confusing. Therefore, the Montessori Method is solidly grounded in reality—the children spend all of their time doing real activities rather than fantasy play. Instead of pretending to cook with plastic food, the children prepare real food. Learning about reality is so important that the classroom even has a specific section, the sensorial area, devoted to helping the children identify reality.

Our apparatus for educating the senses offers the child a key to guide his explorations of the world...[24]

The sensory education which prepares for the accurate perception of

---

24. Maria Montessori, *The Absorbent Mind*, (Clio Press) 183.

all the differential details and the qualities of things, is therefore the foundation of the observation of things and of phenomena which present themselves to our senses; and with this it helps us to collect from the external world the material for the imagination.[25]

Montessori children begin with the concrete perceptions that they are already receiving in reality and are guided in a step-by-step manner toward abstract concepts. They work with hands-on materials most of which have a control of error [26] so that the child can see for himself what is true and what is false. By using these materials, the child also learns that reality is stable; it doesn't change. As the child moves objects around, he can see what happens. If he takes objects away will there be more or less? Will there be less every time? When he counts a quantity, is it stable or will it change? Does 1 + 1 = 2 every time? The child also learns causality (if this happens, that will happen). He begins to understand consequences and starts to learn how to predict outcomes.

An Orderly Mind. Order is a necessary basic component of the ability to think competently; it is easier to think when the mind is in order. It is also the starting point of logic. Order includes the consequences and causality just mentioned in the previous paragraph. Education needs to help the child establish order in his mind.

The child has an unrelenting curiosity. When an astronaut approaches an unknown planet, he has no desire to play with plastic rockets. His only desire is to set his feet upon that planet and explore it. Like the astronaut, the child has discovered existence for the very first time and also has no desire for fantasy play. His only desire is to discover what is in the real world. He explores it, gathers as much information as he can, and accumulates a whirlwind of disconnected information. He then enters into the next stage, his need for order. E. M. Standing, who worked in close collaboration with Dr. Montessori, explains:

> The intellect is the principle of order and mental development. It is of its very essence to create order, and it does so by seeking and binding together like with like, and like with unlike, according to the principles of identity and contrast.

---

25. Maria Montessori, *Spontaneous Activity in Education*, (Robert Bentley) 248.
26. Most of the materials are self-correcting, so that the child can see for himself if he made a mistake.

...

> Although it is true that, by the time he comes to three years of age, the child's intellect has achieved prodigious construction (when compared with the "nothing" with which it started), yet it is also true that there still remains, outside and beyond that part of the world which it has explored and mapped out, a vast and unexplored region where ignorance and confusion still reign. As Montessori puts it: "*The child of three still carries within him a heavy chaos.*" He is still the young explorer, and every day he finds himself constantly coming up against unexplained mysteries, unrelated experiences and puzzling anomalies.
>
> All sorts of ideas and images jostle in his mind without logical connection. (A young friend of mine – aged five – said to his mother: "I sneezed and the clock stopped!") The child's immature intelligence is still as active as ever, trying to extend the bounds of its cosmos at the expense of this inner and outer chaos, endeavoring constantly to bring even more and more objects, facts and experiences under the reign of law and order.
>
> It is a hard task, this, of trying to understand the world in which he lives… Yet the child's mind carries on undaunted in spite of the appalling perplexity of it all.
>
> …the stream of mental energy in the child who has to tackle this work is very limited. And so, our efforts as educators should be directed into helping him to do it as quickly, easily and efficiently as possible.[27]

The child's next conceptual task is to learn how to organize his mind so that he can think clearly. This is why we see three-year-olds who want the same routines, such as the same story read or the same plate at dinner time. This is good because it is necessary for the child to establish stability as he is forming concepts.

> *He constructs his mind step by step till it becomes possessed of memory, the power to understand, the ability to think.*[28]

The child's grasp of order is greatly helped when he learns during his sensitive periods. A sensitive period is the optimum time for the human brain to learn a specific skill. There is a range of time when most children

---

27. E. M. Standing, *The Montessori Method*, 66–67.
28. Maria Montessori, *The Absorbent Mind*, (Dell) 27.

learn how to crawl, walk, and talk. Some children do it a little earlier and some a little later, but if they don't learn it when that part of the brain is most active, it becomes harder to learn later. In his first two years of life, a child learns to speak by absorbing from his environment. Yet an adult would typically need formal instruction were he to visit a foreign country for two years. If a child learns a specific skill when his sensitive period for it is at its peak, he will flow right into it with ease. Just as there are sensitive periods for crawling, walking, and talking, there are sensitive periods for learning how to read, to perform mathematical operations, to develop social skills, to develop concentration, to grasp grammar, and so on. There is even a sensitive period for the brain's method of functioning—it is basically arranged by age six. Just as a building's foundation will determine its strength and success, the foundation of the brain will have a major impact on a person's ability to think and therefore on his success.

When a sensitive period closes down, the next area of the brain opens up for development, as the child enters another sensitive period. The child needs to learn by understanding one layer of knowledge before going onto the next one in the sequence, and he must take his time at each point to fully absorb what he needs for the next one. The brain has its own timetable for development, so the length of time it takes to learn a skill varies from child to child. This is why both putting undue pressure on a child to excel or holding him back in his development is harmful. Our goal as educators is to enrich each stage of development as much as possible to strengthen the brain.

Helping a child build an ordered mind, a mind with a system for organizing facts, is a purpose of a Montessori classroom. As Montessori said, an ordered mind is like a library that is arranged logically, rather than a bunch of books piled up at random.[29]

> It is not the accumulation of a direct knowledge of things which forms the man of letters, the scientist, and the connoisseur; it is the prepared order established in the mind which is to receive such knowledge. On the other hand, the uncultivated person has only the direct knowledge of objects... such a person may be a lady who spends a great part of the night reading books, or a gardener who spends his life making material distinctions between the plants in his garden. The knowledge of such uncultured minds is not only disorderly, but it is confined to the objects with which it comes into direct contact, whereas the knowledge

---

29. Maria Montessori, *Spontaneous Activity in Education*, (Robert Bentley) 203–204.

> *of the scientist is infinite, because, possessing the power of classifying the attributes of things, he can recognize them all, and determine now the class, now the relationships, now the origins of each; facts much more profound than the actual things could of themselves reveal.* [30]

The Montessori materials help the child put his mind in order by isolating one quality at a time. For example, the material for length has ten rods, each one differing in length, but not in color, texture, sound, or any other attribute. When the child learns the names of colors, he uses tablets that are exactly the same except for color. The nomenclature material also isolates one quality at a time when children are learning about first-level concepts. When learning the parts of a tree, for example, the parts are distinguished on separate cards with only one part colored in on each card.[31] Concepts form clearly in the child's mind when the characteristics are isolated because he doesn't get confused by non-essentials.

Order is everywhere in the Montessori classroom. The child can't miss it. There is order in how the room is arranged, order in the work on the shelves, order in the daily routine, order in when work is presented (during the child's sensitive periods), and order in how work is presented. The learning is in logical order, and facts are presented step by step. He is not presented with topics that are way above his grasp. He starts at the concrete level with first-level concepts and works his way up the conceptual ladder step by step, going from simple to hard, each step getting more abstract. The child absorbs this order and thereby puts his mind in order.

Exercising One's Free Will. The ability to reason is reliant upon the ability to use one's free will. The dictionary defines free will as "the doctrine that the conduct of human beings expresses personal choice and is not simply determined by physical or divine forces." [32] Free will is the human capacity to freely select between and among alternatives presented in the environment. To a great degree, we are self-enacting causal agents by our choices, making our lives turn out the way they do—and therefore we are responsible for the actions we take.

---

30. Maria Montessori, *Spontaneous Activity in Education*, (Robert Bentley) 206.

31. This material also prepares the child for reading and writing. He sees a picture (a symbol for a concept) with the word (another symbol for the concept). This helps him to isolate in his mind the idea that each concept has a written symbol.

32. Dictionary.com, "Free will," *Dictionary.com*, 2024.

Thinking is a matter of choice; it isn't possible without exercising one's will. Free will is your ability to make voluntary choices or decisions.

A decision is always the result of a choice.[33]

Choice making is vital to figure something out, consider alternatives, or make connections from one abstraction to another. The choices you make determine your life and character.

Our entire life is a continual exercise of decisions.[34]

If humans had no free will, there would be no human progress, no ability to change one's mind, no such thing as correcting mistakes, and no responsibility for one's actions. There is no doubt that Montessori thought that people have free will. She thought the child must build his reasoning powers with his free will.

A child chooses what helps him to construct himself.[35]

He must also build his independence.

> *The stronger we are in such exercises, the more independent we shall be of others. Clarity of ideas, the mechanism of the habit of decision, gives us a sense of liberty. The heaviest chain, which may bind us in a humiliating form of slavery, is an incapacity to make our own decisions, and the consequent need to refer to others; the fear of making "a mistake," the sense of groping in the dark, of having to bear the consequences of an error we are not certain to recognize, makes us run behind another person like a dog on a chain.*[36]

When the child was an infant his subconscious drove him, and concentrating and learning happened spontaneously, but between the ages of two and three, this process changes. Now he has to develop his will in order to learn by controlling his impulses and inhibitions.

---

33. Maria Montessori, *Spontaneous Activity in Education*, (Robert Bentley) 180.
34. Maria Montessori, *Spontaneous Activity in Education*, (Robert Bentley) 182.
35. Maria Montessori, *The Absorbent Mind*, (Dell) 223.
36. Maria Montessori, *Spontaneous Activity in Education*, (Robert Bentley) 182.

> *It is in the education of the will by means of free exercises wherein the impulses balance the inhibitions that the cure of such subjects might be found, provided such a cure could be undertaken at the age when the will is in process of formation.*[37]

Choice making develops and strengthens will power. As the child makes choices in his work, his will and self-control mature, and he learns how to concentrate. Montessori thought that,

> *The first essential for the child's development is concentration. It lays the whole basis for his character and social behavior.*[38]

The child learns from experience and repetition. It is by choosing a work and repeating it over and over and over that the child learns how to concentrate.

The sensitive period for learning how to concentrate is two to four years of age. The adult has a role in assisting the child as he learns how to concentrate. The teacher needs to present work to the child when he is developmentally ready and the work needs to be purposeful. Once the child begins to concentrate on his work, the teacher needs to fade into the background and allow him to repeat the activity as long as he needs. It is very important that the child not be interrupted, as this is the time that his ability to stay focused is formed.

As explained earlier, by the time a child turns three, his mind has acquired the foundation for knowledge. Now he is ready to put it together, to make sense of his impressions, to make sense of the chaos. He wants to know and is ready to create his "self." He does it by working.

> *Man builds himself through working. Nothing can take the place of work, neither physical well-being nor affection, and, on the other hand, deviations cannot be corrected by either punishment or example. Man builds himself through working, working with his hands, but using his hands as the instruments of his ego, the organ of his individual mind and will, which shapes its own existence face to face with its environment.*[39]

---

37. Maria Montessori, *Spontaneous Activity in Education*, (Robert Bentley) 177.
38. Maria Montessori, *The Absorbent Mind*, (Dell) 222.
39. Maria Montessori, *The Secret of Childhood*, (Montessori-Pierson) 195.

In a Montessori classroom, children have freedom (within limits) to make choices and learn from the choices they make, but the choice making in the classroom is not a free-for-all. The children have rules and guidelines that are consistently enforced, and the child must be academically, physically, and emotionally ready for the choices they make. By evaluating their choices, they learn how to improve their thinking.

Intellectual Independence. Thinking is essentially an issue of intellectual independence, of relying on one's own mind to deal with reality. Independence is the recognition that you are responsible for yourself and therefore must do your own thinking, and make your own judgments, decisions, and choices based on this thinking.

The correctness of your thinking is not guaranteed, of course. You can make errors, but thinking and making mistakes is far preferable to unthinking memorization of facts and acceptance of the conclusions of others. The independent mind can correct honest mistakes; it can go back to reality for the answer. But a mind that knows only how to memorize has been seriously hampered because it doesn't know how to distinguish truth from error and cannot even begin to figure out if what it believes *is* an error.

Children have a natural drive for independence. They want to grow up. They want to dress themselves and do things by themselves. Children feel frustrated and upset when adults continuously dress them, feed them, and wait on them when they are perfectly capable of learning how to do those things. Children need to be allowed to initiate their own activities, repeat their work, and figure things out for themselves.

Adults can hamper the child's desire for independence and often do so unknowingly, by continuously telling him what to do and/or by correcting him by peppering him with answers. When the child is told the answers instead of figuring some work out by himself, the child learns not to question and will continue to memorize what he is told instead of looking at the facts on the ground. If he is told the wrong answers, he will continue to repeat them even when the factual evidence shows otherwise. It is okay to let a child contemplate. Instant answers produce children who want instant gratification and have no patience to wait and think. When adults do too much for the child, when the child's independence is discouraged, he concludes he is incompetent and feels insecure.

Independence is so important that Montessori was opposed to overpraising. Adults often over-praise the child, thinking that praise gives the child self-esteem. No one gets self-esteem from praise; it does not come from approval from others. Self-esteem develops firsthand through work which Montessori recognized,

> *Perfection and confidence must develop in the child from inner sources with which the teacher has nothing to do.*[40]

Self-esteem is earned by developing a competent mind that is able to deal with reality.

Children initially develop their self-evaluation from the conclusions that they draw about the world through their own experiences. If they think reality is understandable and that they are capable of understanding it, they will have a positive view of themselves, but if they think reality is chaos and that they aren't capable of understanding it, they will have a negative view of themselves.

The over-praised child becomes dependent upon being accepted by others which becomes more important to him than the pursuit of knowledge. If independence is discouraged, the child grows up to be dependent on how others define reality. When looking out at the world the dependent person's first thought is, "What do others think is true?" rather than, "What *is* true?" No one can claim to know anything when they just repeat what they have been told or what they have heard. The bottom line of knowledge is reality, and it is only the independent thinker who can discern truth from fiction. Independence and the ability to think go hand in hand. Montessori noted,

> *The child who has never learned to act alone, to direct his own actions, to govern his own will, grows into an adult who is easily led and must always lean on others.*[41]

She went on to say that the independent individual is

> *[one who] through his own efforts is able to perform the actions necessary for his own comfort and development in life, conquers himself, and in so doing, multiplies his abilities and perfects himself as an individual.*[42]

---

40. Maria Montessori, *The Absorbent Mind*, (Dell) 274.
41. Maria Montessori, *Citizen of the World*, 118.
42. Maria Montessori, *The Montessori Method*, (Schocken 1912 translation) 101.

Self-reliance and self-sufficiency are vital for survival and crucial to the happiness of every human being. Consequently, independence is the primary aim of Montessori education.

The first area of the classroom, Practical Life, is where the children learn independence by learning self-care, social graces, care of the environment, and self-control. The Montessori approach works because of its fundamental principle of individualism. Each child progresses at his own rate and is treated as a unique person. The child is allowed to practice and repeat his work as much as is needed in order to master one concept or skill before going on to the next. Due to the limited teacher/student ratio, the child does not get too much adult interference. The teachers refrain from telling children answers to questions that the child can figure out himself. In addition, the child is not impeded in his work by other children because sharing is not forced. Therefore, Montessori children feel secure in knowing that their work will not be trounced upon so they feel comfortable exploring the world. The child has opportunities to be on his own so that he can learn how to think and feel secure in what he knows and comfortable in being alone with his own thoughts and observations.

Jane Healy is an educational psychologist who has spent decades figuring out how the environment affects the developing brain. She has written several books on the topic, one of which is *Endangered Minds: Why Children Don't Think and What We Can Do About It*. She explains why it is important to give children the time they need in order to comprehend what they are learning:

> Children are not allowed to sit and think. They are constantly rammed through a curriculum to see how fast we can move them along. As they're marched from activity to activity, even the schedule of the school day doesn't allow time for anyone to reflect. ... The key word is "understanding," not just a forced march through a set body of subject matters. ... Children who can't reflect and who have never been able to pause long enough to be able to solve a difficult problem are going to be far down on the literacy scale.[43]

The self-correcting materials the children use in Montessori are one of the biggest reasons they develop intellectual independence and self-

---

43. Jane Healy, "An Interview with Jane Healy," *Wild Duck Review*, Review IV, no. 2 (1998).

confidence. No one is there to tell him he is wrong, he can see that for himself, so he tries again and figures it out in the privacy of his own mind. He learns that there is no stigma in being wrong and it's okay to make mistakes along the way while he is learning. He is learning how to figure out what he needs to know rather than memorizing an answer that someone tells him. He is learning *how* to think and he is doing it himself. The Montessori child learns to trust his own mind because he has the freedom to work on his own, at his own pace, with adult guidance, but without adult interference that disrupts his concentration and thought process. And in doing so, he learns that his mind is competent and able to deal with the real world.

For Western Civilization to survive, the human race needs to learn how to think properly. The ability to think is essential not only for man's survival but also for his happiness. I don't know of any educational system other than the Montessori Method that uses a highly specialized, integrated method specifically to teach a child how to use his mind. Maria Montessori discovered what children are and how they really learn. She recognized that to reason, it takes much more than just an accumulation of facts.

> *... if education is always to be conceived along the same antiquated lines of a mere transmission of knowledge, there is little to be hoped from it in the bettering of man's future. For what is the use of transmitting knowledge if the individual's total development lags behind?*[44]

The Montessori Method is a realistic approach to learning based on the true nature of the child, and it works when it is implemented correctly and consistently. Unfortunately, it is being contaminated by social justice.

---

44. Maria Montessori, *The Absorbent Mind*, (Dell) 4.

CHAPTER 2
Social Justice

Progressive Education

The road was paved for the social justice movement in this country years ago by so-called progressive education, the approach used today in most schools, both public and private. Progressive education is not in any way progressive; instead, it is regressive. It is the antithesis of the system of education established in Colonial America, a system called Perennialism, which is based on objective reality and universal truths to develop intellectual skills in their students with reading, writing, and arithmetic.[1] It became a decades-long battle for the minds of our children.

Progressive education in America's schools is based on the ideas of John Dewey (1849–1952), a social determinist and diehard socialist, who loathed individualism and capitalism. Dewey aimed to turn America into a socialist state like the Soviet Union, so, to that end, he created a plan to fundamentally transform education. In 1898, he outlined this plan in an article titled "The Primary-Education Fetich."[2] His plan did not involve teaching children how to think. Instead, it dumbed down children by design.

Dewey did not believe in free will. He thought that the individual is formed by his relationships with others,[3] and that social institutions "are a means of creating individuals."[4] His view was in conflict with that of Montessori, who thought that the child forms himself. "*... the human personality is formed through its own efforts.*"[5] Unlike Montessori who thought that the starting point for a child's development was concentration, he thought the starting point was the child's social life: "I believe that the social life of the child is the basis of concentration,

---

1. Linda Goudsmit, *Space Is No Longer*, 104.
2. John Dewey, "The Primary-Education Fetich," 315–328.
3. John Dewey, *Democracy and Education*, 143.
4. John Dewey, "Reconstruction in Philosophy," *Freeditorial.com*, August 4, 2014.
5. Maria Montessori, *The Secret of Childhood*, (Ballantine) 35.

or correlation, in all his training or growth."[6] Dewey thought that the central purpose of school is not "science, nor literature, nor history, nor geography…but the child's own social activities."

In 1899, in *The School and Society*, John Dewey wrote, "The mere absorbing of facts and truths is so exclusively individual an affair that it tends very naturally to pass into selfishness. There is no obvious social motive for the acquirement of mere learning, there is no clear social gain in success thereat."[7] The book's dominant premise—that the individual should be subordinated to the group—gradually came to be accepted. We can see that in the schools where children are not treated as individuals, and this is taken for granted with no thought given to any other possibility.

Perhaps Dewey's most horrific position was his view of reality. He did not think that objective truth exists. "Quest for certainty that is universal, applying to everything, is a compensatory perversion."[8] It is astounding that people like Dewey can be so certain that there is no such thing as objective reality.

Instead, he thought that truth is whatever the group believes.[9] So, unless there was some social benefit, he viewed the individual pursuit of knowledge as a negative objective and even discouraged it. The purpose of education, according to Dewey, is to socialize children, not to understand the real world.

The idea that "the truth is whatever the group believes" stands against identifying the facts of reality and paralyzes thinking. With this kind of system, relationships take primacy over truth, so, to avoid conflicts among the students, children feel pressured to agree rather than to try to figure out right from wrong or truth from falsehood. The implication is the pursuit of the truth creates trouble, but ignorance creates peace.

This is a serious and upsetting lesson that children are learning. On the one hand they can conclude that there is something wrong with disagreement, that it is anti-social and to be avoided, but on the other, in seeming contradiction, that there are truths. Independent minds some-

---

6. John Dewey, "My Pedagogic Creed," *School Journal*, 77–80.

7. John Dewey, "The School and Social Progress," *The School and Society*, 29.

8. John Dewey, *The Quest for Certainty*, 228.

9. Wikipedia, "Pragmatic theory of truth," *Wikipedia*. Dewey stated in Logic: The Theory of Inquiry that the best definition of truth is that by Peirce: "The opinion which is fated to be ultimately agreed to by all who investigate is what we mean by the truth, and the object represented in this opinion is the real [CP 5.407]. (Dewey, 343 n)."

times disagree with each other. That's okay. That's how progress is made. People disagreed with Galileo when he said the earth went around the sun. People disagreed with the Wright Brothers when they thought man could fly. How do people move forward? Make advancements? Progress and harmony happen when people are free to agree and disagree and act on their independent ideas.

So now, children should not disagree with each other? Reality is agreement with each other? It is not surprising that many people are afraid to say what they really think. They don't want to create waves, so they remain silent to "get along." After all, social relationships are more important than reality, right? And if reality depends on what other people think it is, then they must be correct. Progressive education stamps out the ability to think independently, so people just accept whatever the culture gives them. Without independence of mind, anyone with enough clout can capture and control the entire culture.

In "The Primary-Education Fetich" [10] Dewey stated that the study of the English language should not take place before the age of eight. When teaching a child how to read, his strategy was to eliminate phonics (teaching the sounds of the letters), which led to the look-say method (recognizing words by sight). The problem with Dewey's plan is it sabotages learning. To eliminate phonics and delay reading pushes it beyond the period the child's mind is most receptive to it. Learning to read then becomes so hard that children become bored, discouraged, and/or low-level readers. The colossal failure of the look-say method demonstrates this.[11] Dewey understood the importance of reading, which shows the degree of his debauchery in developing an inferior and unsuccessful method of reading. In his own words:

> Reading and writing were obviously what they are still so often called—the open doors to learning and to success in life. All the meaning that belongs to these ends naturally transferred itself to the means through which alone they could be realized. The intensity and ardor with which our forefathers set themselves to master reading and writing, the difficulties overcome, the interest attached in the ordinary routine of school-life to what now seems barren—the curriculum of the three R's—all testify to the motive-power these studies possessed. To learn to read and write was an interesting, even exciting, thing: it made such a difference in life....[12]

---

10. John Dewey, "The Primary-Education Fetich," 315–328.
11. Emily Hanford, "At a Loss for Words," *APM News Report*, August 22, 2019.
12. John Dewey, "The Primary-Education Fetich," 316–317.

Reading is a gateway to knowledge, and writing is a gateway to thinking. Without reading, learning is severely limited. Dewey knew that reading "made such a difference in life…" Form your own conclusion about what kind of a man he was.

Dewey knew that Americans would not approve of his plan for transformation. "Change must come gradually," he wrote. "To force it unduly would compromise its final success by favoring a violent reaction."[13] Dewey and his Progressives reduced the quality of education on purpose and shielded their sabotage in deception.

By 1909, the Montessori Method was gaining international attention because of the amazing academic progress and independence of the children. Dewey and his followers fought the Montessori movement. Among their criticisms were that the children were taught to read too early, taught to read using phonics, allowed to work alone, and prevented from doing whatever they wanted with the learning materials (they claimed this stifled creativity). However, their greatest objection was that the Montessori child focuses on developing his own individual mind first and foremost. In Montessori's own words:

> *The most important side of human development is the mental side. For man's movements have to be organized according to the guidance and dictation of his mental life. Intelligence is what distinguishes man from the animals, and the building up of his intelligence is the first thing to occur. Everything else waits upon this.*[14]

The result of John Dewey's progressive education is not pretty. Instead of producing students with self-esteem and confidence, it gives us students who are consumed with self-doubt because their thoughts do not come to them first-hand. They feel an unbearable inner state full of fear and helplessness. They stand around with their eyes glazed over, their brains in a fog. Ever wonder why so many teens are depressed? One reason is they are terrified. The world seems unknowable and they have no tools to think, grow, and go out into the world and be productive. Another reason is they are bored to death. The excitement they felt as a young child to explore and learn about the world was stolen from them.

Dewey's final victory comes when students enter college. They hope that they will finally learn something but within the first quarter of their

---

13. John Dewey, "The Primary-Education Fetich," 327.
14. Maria Montessori, *The Absorbent Mind*, (Dell) 72.

freshman year, they find no relief. In philosophy class, the nail is put into the coffin. They are told that their confusion is normal; that reality is unknowable; that there are no absolutes; that what's true for one person isn't true for another; that morality is relative; that if a tree fell in a forest and no one was there to hear it fall, it didn't make a sound.

The students have been abandoned in the confusion about reality that the four-and-five-year-old children in my classroom tried to figure out, and they are left to swim around in their confusion about metaphysics with no hope for even a life jacket for survival. This is not what we want for Montessori. Do we want insecure, sad, inept adults who can't reason their way through life?

Montessori's position that education should be centered around the child's cognitive development is in direct opposition to Dewey's view that education should be centered around social development. Since most of our citizens were educated in progressive schools, Dewey's ideas permeate our culture and are influential everywhere. There are even Montessorians who have accepted the antithetical notion that children are created by their social relationships instead of their work. Any Montessorian who has instituted social justice, which is group based, into his/her classroom has abandoned the Montessori Method, and by extension, has abandoned the child.

What is Social Justice?

Morally, justice is the recognition of the fact that you judge individuals according to their virtues and/or vices and treat them accordingly. Social justice, however, is the idea that justice is attained through social structures or groups. It puts people into groups based on race, sex, skin color, etc. It then places groups higher than individuals, and holds that all groups should be equal. If there are any disparities in group outcomes, they are attributed to discrimination and group injustice rather than individual choices and actions, and therefore the more successful groups need to be punished. This results in groups constantly fighting each other. The average person mistakenly thinks social justice is all about equality and fairness, but it is actually about collectivism, the suppression of the individual in favor of the group. The individual has no identity—no character, no qualities, no morality—outside of his group membership. In truth, therefore, "social justice" is the opposite of justice.

The American ideal of justice is that of individual justice—equality under the law regardless of group affiliation. There is no other kind. If individuals work to earn their living, they can keep the fruits of their labor. If individuals violate the rights of others (stealing, murder, etc.), the violators go to jail. There is no guilt by association. There is no presumed guilt without evidence based on social factors. Philosophically, American culture values judging people by their actions and the content of their character, or used to. Social justice, however, seeks to reward or punish groups based on their collective memberships.

Justice only applies to individuals. To add the modifier "social" is an attempt to change the meaning of justice from what one has earned and equality under the law to its opposite, equity. Equity means each group must be made equal regardless of its individual members having earned it. That logically requires the use of force to take from one person to benefit another. This is the very antithesis of justice.

Social justice makes another unfair claim. It says certain groups are inherently racist. Robin DiAngelo, a consultant, educator, and facilitator for over 20 years on issues of racial and social justice, makes just such a claim. Her book, *White Fragility: Why It's So Hard for White People to Talk About Racism,* was released in 2018 and was on the New York Times Bestseller List for more than three years. DiAngelo thinks there is no such thing as free will; that people are determined by their race or social structure. In her book she says, "White identity is inherently racist; white people do not exist outside the system of white supremacy."[15] And, "A racism free upbringing is not possible, because racism is a social system embedded in the culture and its institutions. We are born into the system and have no say in whether we will be affected by it."[16] And, "It is not possible to be free of prejudice."[17]

There are times when judgment based on group affiliation is appropriate, such as when someone joins a group voluntarily because of its ideological position. In that case, one can reasonably conclude that its members agree with its position. For example, one can say that most church-goers believe in God. By contrast, DiAngelo formed conclusions about a group of people (white people), not based on the ideals they have chosen, but based on the color of their skin. The author has a right

---

15. Robin DiAngelo, *White Fragility*, 148.
16. Ibid.
17. Ibid.

to speak for herself, as does anyone, but not for a group of people who had no choice in their physical characteristics. People, like DiAngelo, who see themselves only as a member of a group because of the color of their skin rather than individuals with their own thoughts, will think all people with the same skin color think the same way.

A definition of racism is in order here. Racism claims that a person is determined by physical factors out of his control, such as skin color. It holds that a person's values and the content of his mind is either determined before birth or by his social group. Social justice activists hold that people are even responsible for things that their ancestors did hundreds of years ago. That is the very definition of racism.

Montessori disagrees with the idea that racism is innate.

> *By taking the child into consideration we touch something common to all humanity. We cannot achieve world harmony simply by attempting to unite all these adult people who are so different; but we can achieve it if we begin with the child who is not born with national and racial prejudices.*

Racism is deterministic; it says you are determined to think a certain way based on your skin color, race, or sex; and it rejects free will. To say that a group is inherently evil means that no one in that group has any choice as to his character or actions. A person cannot change because he has no control over who he is. This idea of racism does not recognize any ability of a person to think for himself, come to his own conclusions, and form his own character. Yet, in truth, it is only through the use of his reasoning powers that the child is able to understand the difference between good and evil and make a choice between them. Racism, or any other crude form of collectivist judgment, is the cruel and evil form of judging and relating to others.

Montessori most definitely supported the idea that the child creates himself by using his free will.

> *What matters is not physics or botany, or works of the hand, but the will, and the components of the human spirit which construct themselves by work.*[18]

> *The very fact that a child is not subject to fixed and predetermined*

---
18. Maria Montessori, *The Absorbent Mind*, (Clio Montessori Press) 221.

guiding instincts is an indication of its innate liberty and freedom of action.[19]

The antidote to racism is individualism. Individualism is the doctrine that the interests of the individual are ethically paramount, that all values and rights originate in individuals, and that human conduct should be guided by such a doctrine. It emphasizes the moral worth of the individual. An individual is self-reliant. He develops his own character by his own thinking and his own choices.

Montessori viewed the individual child as the most important part of the education process:

The educator must be as one inspired by a deep worship of life, and must, through this reverence, respect, while he observes with human interest, the development of the child's life… There exists only one real biological manifestation: the living individual; and toward single individuals, one by one observed, education must direct itself.[20]

She thought that the starting point in education was the individual child himself, not the group:

This child who stands before us with his marvelous hidden energies must lead our efforts. When we say that the child is our teacher, we mean that we must take his revelations as our guide. Our starting point must be the revelation of the characteristics of the human individual.[21]

The nature of this educational work begins to take shape. It consists in cultivating the immense potential of the individual in order that his hidden energies may develop wholesomely.[22]

She even said that when the child learns how to command his will, it expresses his individuality, not just the characteristics of human groups:

Nature conditions the child otherwise than the young of animals. She leaves the realm of movement free from the imperious despotism of instinct. Instinct withdraws; the muscles wait, strong and obedient, for

---

19. Maria Montessori, *The Secret of Childhood*, (Ballantine) 31.
20. Maria Montessori, *The Discovery of the Child*, 104.
21. Maria Montessori, *The 1946 London Lectures*, vol. 17.
22. Maria Montessori, *Citizen of the World*, 76.

a new order; they await the command of the will to co-ordinate them in the service of the human spirit. They must express the characteristics not of a mere species, but of an individual soul. [23]

Montessori's view of individualism is incongruent with the social justice movement that views people as groups, rather than individuals. The child in Montessori is not viewed primarily as a group member. The child is neither created by the group, nor is he determined by the group.

Placing groups above individuals is devastating. If a child is told that he is racist because of the color of his skin, and he believes it, he will cower in shame. If pressure is put upon him to agree that he is a racist by his teachers or friends, it will cause his reasoning skills to collapse in fear. Then he will feel the need to "fit in" somewhere to feel worthwhile and accepted. He will begin to feel frightened of other children as he fears rejection based on his skin color or other obtuse reason. You will see children form gangs, just like in the progressive schools, and those gangs will fight with each other, then the peace that we have seen in our classrooms will disappear. If children are taught social justice doctrines, to regard each other as groups with pre-determined racist or other group characteristics rather than individuals with their own chosen behaviors, it will kill the Montessori Method.

Education is decidedly instrumental in influencing children's attitudes towards racism. Education needs to center around developing the child as an individual as Montessori said. When the child is viewed as an individual, is treated as an individual, and is educated as an individual, children end up viewing each other as individual, independent persons rather than as members of different races.

Marxism

Social justice is not new. It originated at the Frankfurt School in Germany in the 1920s [24] where the ideology of Karl Marx (1818–1883) was taught and expanded upon. (The Frankfurt School's original intended name was actually the Institute of Marxism.[25]) It was here that Critical Theory, a theory that criticizes modern society, was born. By holding that reason,

---

23. Maria Montessori, *The Secret of Childhood*, (Montessori-Pierson) 29.
24. Valaida (Val) L. Wise, "Critical Race Theory," *American Montessori Society*.
25. William Lind, "Chapter VI Further Readings on the Frankfurt School," *Commons. wikimannia.org*.

the foundation of Western Civilization, stood in the way of provoking a socialist revolution, the Frankfurt School condemned Western culture. To put it another way, they went about trying to destroy Western Civilization because they viewed reason as a threat.[26]

Karl Marx was a German-born political philosopher and revolutionary. He and Friedrich Engels (1820–1895) wrote the *Communist Manifesto*, the platform for communism. Communism is a political ideology where the state owns and controls the means of production. There is no private property and the stated goal is to seize the wealth from those who produce it and then redistribute it. The goal is power and control over those who produce. In other words, theft and enslavement.

The Communist Manifesto, written in 1847, held that, throughout history, society has had constant struggles between the oppressors and the oppressed which ends in revolution. In feudal eras, there was constant conflict between several classes, the higher ones and the lower ones. The society that evolved after feudalism had two classes—Bourgeoisie and Proletariat, the producers/traders and the workers. Marx thought that capitalism was erected to give power to the bourgeoisie and organize society to exclude everybody else.

There was one major problem. Marx was wrong. The Neo-Marxists came to admit that capitalism did not immiserate the worker. Therefore, the working class was no longer to be the base of the Marxist revolution.[27]

Logan Lansing, author of *The Queering of the American Child*, explains:

> In fact, by the 1960s, critical Marxists like Herbert Marcuse and Max Horkheimer [prominent members of the Frankfurt School] were admitting that "advanced capitalism" "delivers the goods" and "allows [workers] to build a better life," one "to be sure" is a "good life."
>
> ...
>
> In other words, the communist revolution was no longer inevitable; the worker was no longer likely to be its vehicle; and Marxists needed new tools to push us all towards the end of History.[28]

---

26. Timothy Matthews, "The Frankfurt School: Conspiracy to Corrupt," *Catholic Insight*, 1–4.

Timothy Matthews, "Frankfurt School," *World Book Encyclopedia*.

27. James Lindsay, "Woke: A Culture War Against Europe," *NewDiscourses.Subtack.com*, March 29, 2023.

28. Logan Lansing, *The Queering of the American Child*, 58.

Therefore, the neo-Marxists had to figure out other ways to destabilize society so that they could take power. They used Critical Theory, which ruthlessly criticizes current society. They created constant conflict over the contrived issue of oppression through various movements, one of which was social justice.

On January 10, 1963, forty-five communist goals for taking over the United States were read into the Congressional Record by Congressman Albert S. Herlong Jr., (D-Florida).[29] The goals were taken from the testimony of scholars and from the writings of communists. Here are a few of those goals which would cause decline and destabilize our country:

1. Get control of the schools. Use them as transmission belts for Socialism and current Communist propaganda. Soften the curriculum.

2. Present homosexuality, degeneracy and promiscuity as "normal, natural and healthy."

3. Break down cultural standards of morality by promoting pornography and obscenity in books, magazines, motion pictures, radio, and TV.

4. Use student riots to foment public protests against programs or organizations which are under Communist attack.

5. Belittle all forms of American culture and discourage the teaching of American history.

6. Discredit the family as an institution. Encourage promiscuity and easy divorce.

7. Emphasize the need to raise children away from the negative influence of parents. Attribute prejudices, mental blocks and retarding of children to suppressive influence of parents.

8. Discredit the American Constitution by calling it inadequate, old fashioned, out of step with modern needs, a hindrance to cooperation between nations on a worldwide basis.

9. Discredit the American founding fathers. Present them as selfish aristocrats who had no concern for the "common man."

---

29. Congressional Record, *Congressional Record — House,* January 10, 1963.
Donna Calvin, "The 45 Communist Goals," *Belief Net,* January 10, 1963.

It is frightening to observe that communists have made quite a bit of progress with these goals. Note the ones concerning children. Why do you suppose Marxists want to get control of the schools, sexualize and separate children from their parents, and use students for riots?

Marxists have known for a long time that the way to spark revolutions is through education of the youth. Marcuse explains:

> To extend the face of the student movement, Rudi Dutschke has proposed the strategy of the *long march through the institutions*: working against the established institutions while working in them, but not simply by "boring from within," rather by "doing the job," learning how to program and read computers, how to teach at all levels of education, how to use the mass media, how to organize production, how to recognize and eschew obsolescence, how to design, etc. and at the same time preserving one's own consciousness and working with the others.[30]

Neo-Marxists aren't the first or only ones who know the power of education. Lenin created Marxist schools to teach students that "the entire purpose of their lives is to build a communist society."[31] Yuri Bezmenov, a former KGB propagandist who defected to the West, explained that the first step in taking over the United States is ideological subversion, a process of brainwashing three generations of students to favor Marxism.[32] Montessori was also well aware that early influences on children have a big impact on the future of a country.

> *To change a generation of nation, to influence it towards either good or evil, to re-awaken religion or add culture, we must look to the child, who is omnipotent. The truth of this has been demonstrated of late by Nazis and Fascists, who changed the character of a whole peoples by working on children.*[33]

Paulo Freire

Political activists took over American education following a plan for teaching social justice devised by Paulo Freire (1921–1997), a Brazilian

---

30. James Lindsay, *The Marxification of Education*, 22–23.
31. Vladimir Lenin, "The tasks of the youth leagues," *Marxist Internet Archive*, 1999.
32. Yuri Bezmenov, "Yuri Bezmenov - How To Demoralize A Nation," *YouTube*, June 21, 2020.
33. Maria Montessori, *Education For A New World*, 34.

educator and philosopher. It's a plan used widely in schools today. Freire was a leading advocate of a branch of Critical Theory called Critical Pedagogy, an educational method that encourages students to examine power structures and patterns of inequality through an "awakening" in pursuit of freedom from oppression. Freire took Dewey's quasi-Marxist ideas of school reform a step further, and it has had a major impact. Freire's book, *Pedagogy of the Oppressed*, is given an important position in virtually every education program in North America today. In it he explains his basic principles of education, which are essentially Marxist. The goal is to abolish formal education and objective knowledge and, instead, foster learning to see oppression in virtually everything so that it can be denounced. It is a process of becoming politically aware of a hidden, horrific world of the social justice crusaders' own creation. Becoming literate is secondary to becoming politically literate.[34]

One of the means to turn children political is through a subtle form of indoctrination that uses a "generative themes" approach. A generative theme is using something that matters to a student in order to manipulate him. This is done by evoking his emotions about a topic he cares about and then provoking emotional discussions. James Lindsay, in his book *The Marxification of Education*, describes this method:

> A particular angle on this might be to try to get students to explain what it would feel like to be, say, a poor black person who believes the reason they are poor is systemic or structural racism. This forces the children to enter into a state of believing systemic racism is *real* instead of a particular (and purposed) interpretation of the world *through their emotions,* which easily deny logic and evidence.[35]

The children do not learn anything more about the subject, poverty, in this example, from a different viewpoint. They only hear the side of someone who ostensibly feels oppressed. Then they are shown data and pictures of people suffering. Through guided discussion, the teacher leads the children to conclude that the oppressor is society and/or the system of capitalism. The learners, who by now are emotionally charged, feel that something must be done to alleviate the suffering of the victim. The teacher then asks them to identify as the victims (decodification) whether by race, sex, class, sexuality, skin color, etc. The students then start to

---

34. James Lindsay, *The Marxification of Education*, 21–39.
35. James Lindsay, *The Marxification of Education*, 135.

see themselves as victims and can join the oppressed in the struggle for revolution.[36] In most cases, the children are not even conceptually ready to learn about politics, so from an early age, they are conditioned to have a negative emotional reaction to a topic and then form conclusions because of that emotion.

Freire's goal for teaching social justice in education is to convince children that they belong to some oppressed group, ensure class (group) struggles and conflict, and thereby change innocent children into activists. Children who have been educated under progressive education can easily fall prey to the notion that they are oppressed. Having learned that there are no absolutes, and lacking the ability to reason, they are unable to think and judge. Therefore, they feel inadequate to deal with reality and lack self-confidence. Surely, oppression is the reason why they feel inept and unhappy. Insecurity is what lures children (and adults) into cults and deceit.

Queer Theory

Another Marxist tactic used to destabilize children is to turn them "queer." Queer in this context comes from Queer Theory,[37] another offshoot of Critical Theory that asserts sexual norms are oppressive and anything normal is a problem. In 1984, Gayle Rubin, a leading queer theorist, wrote a founding document for queer theory called "Thinking Sex."[38] Queer theory includes, but is not limited to, the following:

- Queer means an identity without an essence, or to be outside the norm.
- Queer theory opposes normality and ethics with regards to sex—everything must be opened up or it is oppression.
- In order for the child to develop outside of reality, the adult should eliminate all boundaries.
- Children are oppressed by adults who think that "cross generational encounters" (in other words pedophilia) are horrors.
- Exposure to sexual acts is fine for children (anyone under the legal age of consent).

---

36. Logan Lancing, *The Queering of the American Child*, 122–126.
37. James Lindsay, "Queer Theory," *New Discourses*, April 7, 2020.
38. Richard Parker, *Culture Society and Sexuality*.

- Children need to be seen as equal to adults. Therefore, they can consent to sex.
- Child pornography is fine and there should be no laws restricting it.
- It is a "considerable burden" for sadomasochists and pedophiles to maintain absolute secrecy about their real sexual identities.
- There should be no separation between "adult" sexuality and childhood "innocence."
- The child should not be kept racially or sexually innocent.
- Every child should be treated as if they are queer and kept queer so they are an outcast and can be utilized for revolution.

Ronald Pisaturo, author of *Masculine Power; Feminine Beauty*,[39] a book that explains the history of the LGBT movement, defines a queer as "an activist dedicated to overthrowing capitalism, the system alleged to enforce oppressive sexual norms such as masculinity, femininity, and heterosexuality." Turning children into Marxist activists is the goal of the LGBT movement. Why? Because capitalism has not actually produced a proletariat motivated to revolt as predicted by Marxist theory, so Herbert Marcuse advocated creating a plethora of other discontented groups to revolt, one of which is sexual "queers." This goal is supported by the LGBT ideology that developed under Critical Theory. Pisaturo explains (p. 113) that, according to LGBT theory,

> Infants are "polymorphously perverse," to use Freud's term. That is, an infant will be sexually excited by anyone and anything anywhere. Freud considered this infantile state an early stage of development. Marcuse and many LGBT activists, in contrast, consider this state the ideal end state for adults. According to Marcuse, people leave this ideal state only because they become repressed, limiting the kinds of sexual responses available to them. The repressed energy of such people becomes channeled into economic production… That is, productive work is the repressed alternative to blissful, indiscriminate sex. Capitalism, of course the system of greatest economic production, is hence also the system of greatest sexual repression …

Therefore, capitalism must be destroyed.

Queer activists think that the purpose of education is to change the world through revolution. It cannot be overemphasized. Queer pedagogy

---
39. Ronald Pisaturo, *Masculine Power, Feminine Beauty*.

attacks the child's mind by deconstructing [confusing, dismantling] it, thus making the child unable to think and vulnerable to political programming. The activists are opposed to teaching phonics and math tables because they think these educational programs stabilize society—which is the opposite of what they want. So, learning how to read, write, and do math can't be done in a normal, neutral manner. Instead, reading and math should be done for "social justice." One must ignore math and focus on eliminating oppression. Reading should be practiced to read the "unstated dominant ideologies hidden between the sentences."[40]

A goal of Queer Pedagogy is to push the child into a personal crisis by teaching him that the world is full of malice,[41] that there is no normality in reality, and that he is abnormal. Logan Lansing explains:

> Simply put, Queer Activists convince kids that they can't identify as normal boys or girls – they must choose political positions and enter into an *identity crisis*. Queer Activists must first persuade kids to see themselves as different by "forcing a separation of their sense of self from a sense of normalcy."[42] They are then led to feel as though they are oppressed because they are abnormal. Only then can kids be taught the key reversal that activates them: that they are abnormal because they are oppressed. That is, they would be "normal" too if it weren't for society's expectations to be normal in other terms. Society, by failing to accommodate their quirks, is making them abnormal.[43]

Dr. Kevin Kumashiro, an internationally recognized expert on educational policy regarding equity and social justice approves of pushing children into crisis:

> Once in a crisis, a student can go in many directions, some that may lead to anti-oppressive change, others that may lead to more entrenched resistance. Therefore, educators have a responsibility not only to draw students into a possible crisis, but also to structure experiences that can help them work through their crises productively.[44]

"Productively" in this context means "to push children to develop their character and identity through the lens of queer theory."[45]

---

40. Kincheloe, J. L., *Critical Pedagogy Primer*, 16.
41. Logan Lansing, *The Queering of the American Child*, 141.
42. Kevin Kumashiro, *Troubling Education*, 44.
43. Logan Lansing, *The Queering of the American Child*, 135.
44. K. K. Kumashiro, "Against repetition," *Harvard Educational Review* 72, no. 1 (2002).
45. Logan Lansing, *The Queering of the American Child*, 138.

Child abuse as defined by federal law is "any recent act or failure to act on the part of a parent or caretaker, which results in death, serious physical or emotional harm, sexual abuse or exploitation" or "an act or failure to act which presents an imminent risk of serious harm."[46] Purposefully attempting to damage a child, as is done in queer pedagogy, is child abuse, and furthermore it is wicked. As Logan Lancing said, "This is *not* education. This is *thought reform*. This is systematized *brainwashing*."[47] (Incidentally, "inclusion," which is touted to be a virtue of social justice, does not include children who keep their sense of normalcy because they might make others feel "unsafe."[48])

The efforts to obliterate the self-esteem of children is intentionally hidden from the parents. At the same time the children are taught to expect rejection from their parents because of their new queer identities. The activists are doing everything in their power to destroy the parent-child relationship. They know that for their plan to work, they must sever the special bond between children and parents.

Attempts to destroy a child's sense of normalcy or to destroy the recognition of what is normal are in direct conflict with Montessori's pedagogy that seeks to extinguish any childhood deviations through the process of normalization. Being normal is not oppressive. Normality results in a healthy psychology of peace and productivity. Here is a key Montessori passage where she defines normal.

> *What is to be particularly noted in these child conversions is a psychic cure, a return to what is normal. Actually, the normal child is one who is precociously intelligent, who has learned to overcome himself and to live in peace, and who prefers a disciplined task to feudal idleness. When we see a child in this light, we would more properly call his "conversion" a "normalization." Man's true nature lies hidden within himself. And this nature, which was given him at conception, must be recognized and allowed to grow.*[49]

> *In a child the normal psychic traits can flourish easily. Then all those traits that deviated from the norm disappear, just as with the return of health all the symptoms of a disease vanish.*[50]

---

46. Child Welfare Information Gateway, "Child Abuse and Neglect," *ChildWelfare.org*.
47. Logan Lancing, *The Queering of the American Child*, 135.
48. Logan Lancing, *The Queering of the American Child*, 217.
49. Maria Montessori, *The Secret of Childhood*, (Ballantine) 148.
50. Ibid.

This is very important. Montessori's pedagogy is a rebuke of the nihilistic view that the child should grow up and do whatever he pleases like a little savage as if that's self-actualization. Not even just a savage with no rules, but breaking his own nature.

Queer pedagogy does the opposite. It creates chaos out of order with the goal of creating abnormality, whereas the Montessori Method helps the child to create order out of chaos with the goal of fostering normality.

Thus, we may justly say that to help the development of the intelligence is to help to put the images of the consciousness in order.[51]

The consciousness may possess a rich and varied content; but when there is mental confusion, the intelligence does not appear.[52]

Montessori listed qualities of the normal child that included a firm attachment to reality and a love of order and maintaining it.[53] She esteemed the normal child.

One of the most remarkable characteristics of a "normal" child is his self-confidence and sureness in action.[54]

Unfortunately, there are some Montessori schools that have veered sharply away from Montessori's vision. An article published about one such Montessori high school in *The Advocate* on May 13, 2024, titled, "The queerest education in America: How LGBTQ+ kids thrive at this Indiana school," describes the school as "a beacon of progressive education." It has a staff of eight teachers, five of whom identify as queer. The school centers around fitting in. "It's about socially and emotionally preparing our students for life," said a gay English and humanities teacher. Discussions of gender identity and sexual orientation are held openly, and students have access to books which have been banned in conservative jurisdictions. Flags such as the progress pride flag, the nonbinary pride flag, the transgender pride flag, and a Black Lives Matter flag are displayed next to the United States flag. Nothing in the article indicated an increase in student self-confidence based on the Montessori virtues of independent thinking,

---

51. Maria Montessori, *Spontaneous Activity in Education*, (Robert Bentley) 202.
52. Ibid.
53. E. M. Standing, *Maria Montessori Her Life and Work*, 175–178.
54. Maria Montessori, *The Secret of Childhood*, (Ballantine) 170.

increased knowledge of reality, intellectual pursuits, or creative work. It was all about social acceptance.[55]

Lexington Montessori School in Massachusetts has an entire page on their website devoted to "Social Justice." When you scroll down, you see children with pride flags and this description:

> Lesbian, Gay, Bisexual, Transgender and Queer (LGBTQ) Pride Month is celebrated each year in the month of June to honor the 1969 Stonewall Uprising in Manhattan.[56] At LMS, students across all levels celebrate Pride Day at school. Elementary and Middle School students march in a mini-parade around campus as their Toddler and Children's House peers watch and cheer with excitement.[57]

Social development is not a primary in Montessori, yet the social justice movement, which they follow, focuses on social development first and foremost. There have been claims that they are just teaching kids not to bully classmates who are different. Their method doesn't work even for that. First, they are teaching kids that some people are racists because of the color of their skin. The risk is the children with the "wrong" color skin can feel inferior and shame, and the children with the "right" color skin can feel superior and smug. The right color crowd can easily become the bully crowd and often does. Second, the social justice activists are operating on the premise that all children bully other children who are different. That is false, as people can observe for themselves when they visit a well-run, authentic Montessori school based on individuality instead of racism.

Drag Queens [58]

Queer pedagogy leads to another theory of education—"drag pedagogy." Drag pedagogy is explained in an academic paper entitled "Drag Peda-

---

55. Christopher Wiggins, "The queerest education in America," *The Advocate*, May 13, 2024.
56. History.com, "Stonewall Riots," *History.com*. The Stonewall Uprising in 1969 was riots that were triggered by police when they raided the Stonewall Inn, a gay club in New York, and hauled out patrons and employees.
57. Lexington Montessori School, Lexington, Massachusetts, "Lexington Montessori School," *Lexington Montessori School*.
58. Charlotte Cushman, "The Real Purpose of Drag Queen Story Hour," *American Thinker*, January 22, 2023. This chapter is based on the article printed in the American Thinker.

gogy: The Playful Practice of Queer Imagination in Early Childhood," [59] that was published online in *Curriculum Inquiry*, an educational journal, on January 25, 2021. It was written by Harper Keenen and Lil Miss Hot Mess, a founder of Drag Queen Story Hour (DQSH), who describe themselves as "a genderqueer drag performer/scholar and a trans scholar." [60]

Drag pedagogy advocates exposing children to drag queens, not for entertainment and fun and not to learn about gay culture, but to learn how to live queerly. The abstract of "Drag Pedagogy" confirms this:

> Ultimately, the authors propose that 'drag pedagogy' provides a performative approach to queer pedagogy that is not simply about LGBT lives, but *living queerly*.[61]

> Through this programme, drag artists… [are] positioning queer and trans cultural forms as valuable components of early childhood education. We are guided by the following question: what might Drag Queen Story Hour offer educators as a way of bringing queer ways of knowing and being into the education of young children? [62]

An implicit objective of DQSH is acknowledged explicitly:

> There is a premium on standing out, on artfully desecrating the sacred. [63]

It is, obviously, overtly sexual. Drag Queens are not the joke-telling Cher impersonators of old. They do not want to broaden or enrich the sacred (sexuality) through some kind of deeper understanding, nor are they attempting to be funny besequined clowns. They want to desecrate, to vandalize, to destroy, and they want to do this in children's minds. This is obvious when one observes how women are portrayed by drag queens. Men portray women as bulging, gross, ugly beings dressed up in over-styled inadequate skimpy clothing, with exaggerated features such as caked make up, spiked high heels, etc. They don't dress like real women. They look like prostitutes, swaying, gyrating, and shoving their bodies in a sexually provocative manner, in exactly the manner of strip-

---

59. Harper Keenan, "Drag Pedagogy," *Curriculum Inquiry 50, no. 5 (2020)*.
60. Harper Keenan, "Drag Pedagogy," *Curriculum Inquiry 50, no. 5 (2020)*, 443.
61. Harper Keenan, "Drag Pedagogy," *Curriculum Inquiry 50, no. 5 (2020)*, 440.
62. Ibid.
63. Harper Keenan, "Drag Pedagogy," *Curriculum Inquiry 50, no. 5 (2020)*, 451.

pers, flinging their private body parts around, thereby dragging sexuality through the muck.

During DQSH, drag queens often read sexually inappropriate and/or explicit books to children. Drag queen shows denigrate women and portray sexuality as ugly and cheap and boundaryless. Unfortunately, not only have children been taken to some of these shows, they have even participated in them by stripping, whereupon the adults reward them with money.[64]

The child finds inappropriate and shocking exposure to sex confusing and frightening. A degrading introduction to sex can make a child feel anxious. It separates the sex act from valuing and loving another person and it portrays the people involved as mindless pieces of meat. It separates the mind and body—and the shock and confusion can block out thinking altogether.

The goal of exposing children to drag queen shows is to push them into abnormal sexuality by promoting it through imagery and social pressure and by pushing sexuality in their face everywhere. If children are confused sexually, then when they grow up, they will think that the weird is normal. Children are being exploited shamelessly for the sake of revolutionary ideology. This is despicable.

The "Drag Pedagogy" paper tells us more disturbing things,

> It may be that DQSH is "family friendly," in the sense that it is accessible and inviting to families with children, but it is less a sanitizing force than it is a preparatory introduction to alternate modes of kinship [meaning non-blood "family," not the parents or siblings or other relations]. Here, DQSH is "family friendly" in the sense of "family" as an old-school queer code to identify and connect with other queers on the street.[65]

Pisaturo explains, "The phrase 'preparatory introduction to alternate modes of kinship' means sexual and Marxist grooming. The authors want to eradicate the traditional family by grooming children to join the 'family' of queers."[66]

Attempting to turn children into queers and separating them from

---

64. Mary Rooke, "'Look At All That Money You Just Made!'," *The Daily Caller*, August 3, 2022.

65. Harper Keenan, "Drag Pedagogy," *Curriculum Inquiry 50, no. 5 (2020)*, 455.

66. Charlotte Cushman, "The Real Purpose of Drag Queen Story Hour," *American Thinker*, January 22, 2023.

their family of origin is bad enough, but there are other alarming elements to DQSH. Drag queens teach the children that reality is fluid:

> Drag similarly breaks boundaries between reality and fantasy in allowing performers to take on new identities and social relationships in material form, just by playing the part.[67]

Bringing drag queens into the classrooms of young children is a generative (Freirean) approach as discussed earlier. The drag queens generate themes that are necessary to lead children into dialogues about sex, gender, and sexuality. This enables the instructors to insert empathy and confusion where they desire.

> At many DQSH events, children ask genuine questions like "are you a boy or a girl?" ... In many cases, drag queens may not respond with answers, but with questions meant to complicate perceptions of gender and society: "why does it matter if I'm a boy or a girl?"[68]

The answer matters a great deal to the child who is just beginning to learn about reality and to form concepts. The first judgment anyone perceives about another person is: is the person a girl or a boy? Man or woman? To a child, to destroy that demarcation and bring in the arbitrary, that a man can be a woman, is to undermine the important, fundamental concept of reality: that reality is stable and cannot be wished away. Serious cognitive damage is done by blurring the child's grasp of reality. For the child, an unstable reality confuses him, frightens him, and sabotages his ability to navigate the world.

These practices also teach children to be defiant, not for a valid reason, but for the sake of defiance.

> While drag has some conventions, it ultimately has no rules – its defining quality is often to break as many rules as possible![69]

And this is disturbing:

> She is less interested in focus, discipline, achievement, or objectives than

---

67. Harper Keenan, "Drag Pedagogy," *Curriculum Inquiry 50, no. 5 (2020)*, 449.
68. Harper Keenan, "Drag Pedagogy," *Curriculum Inquiry 50, no. 5 (2020)*, 452.
69. Harper Keenan, "Drag Pedagogy," *Curriculum Inquiry 50, no. 5 (2020)*, 448.

playful self-expression. Her pedagogy is rooted in pleasure and creativity borne, in part, from letting go of control.[70]

The authors are not teaching children how to use their minds to reach their full potential, even their creative potential. Instead, they are teaching children to be abnormal, to be queer, and to be deviants—all for the sake of turning them into pawns to tear down the normal. Remember, Montessori was a proponent of normality.

And the more a man's inner life shall have grown <u>normally</u>, organizing itself in accordance with the provident laws of nature, and forming an individuality, the more richly will he be endowed with a strong will and a well-balanced mind.[71]

Do people really think that it is harmless to bring children to see sexuality portrayed, not as a sacred expression of love for one special individual, but as frivolous "desecrating" for the benefit of any and all strangers? To see sexuality divorced from thought and romance? To see sexuality portrayed as ugly caricature? To see sexuality, which is intensely personal, selective, and meaningful, made voyeuristic, indiscriminate, and meaningless? The young child learns from observation, he learns from absorbing his environment. Everything that he sees and experiences makes an impression upon his mind before he has the ability to evaluate it. The "desecrating" of sexuality will make a child's mind abnormal regarding sex and all cognition, and that is exactly the goal of the drag queens. DQSH and drag shows aren't baseless, and they aren't harmless. They are precisely child abuse.

It is very disturbing to learn that there are Montessori schools that have either hosted drag queen performances or story hours, have incorporated drag culture into their curriculum, have participated in events celebrating drag queens, and/or have promoted drag queens. Some of these locations of schools are in Minnesota,[72] Colorado,[73] Massachusetts,[74]

---

70. Harper Keenan, "Drag Pedagogy," *Curriculum Inquiry 50, no. 5 (2020)*, 451.

71. Maria Montessori, *Spontaneous Activity in Education*, (Robert Bentley) 168.

72. Lake Harriet Montessori School, "Lake Harriet Montessori School," *Lake Harriet Montessori School*.

73. Jarrow Montessori School, "Diversity Resources," *Jarrow Montessori School*.

74. Greater Haverhill Chamber, "June Art Walk celebrates pride," *Greater Haverhill Chamber*. See Wisteria Montessori School.

Florida,[75] and New York.[76] Doubtless there are more. These schools need to stop this participation immediately.

In addition to trying to turn children queer, exposing them to the disgusting behavior of drag queens is an attempt to sexualize them. Sexualizing occurs when children are regarded as sex objects and/or are encouraged to be sexual. Sexualizing can include, but is not limited to, continuously drawing attention to sex, approving or encouraging sex transitioning, inappropriately exposing children to sex, participating in sexual events or actions such as drag queen shows, and using books showing pornography, including sex acts such as oral sex and masturbation.[77]

Some Montessori schools are implementing Queer Pedagogy by sexualizing children. On the New Discourses website, I found a mother quite upset with her child's Montessori school in Minnesota:

> Our quaint K–8 Montessori school has implemented heavy handed gender identity lessons and disturbing changes to the reproductive health lessons and materials. The upper elementary (4–6th grade) received several hours of reproductive lessons. They are using books in the classrooms (1–3rd grade and 4–6th grade, all mixed age classes) by author Cory Silverberg, who, I recently learned, founded a sex shop "Come as You Are." The sex store "for beginners" uses the same graphics, font, colors as used in his books for children. The sex shop matches his children's books. One page of his book says that when a baby is born the doctor guesses the gender and can mistake a "large clitoris for a small penis or a small penis for a large clitoris." For 10 to 12-year-olds. This is one example of several messages in the book, *Sex is a Funny Word*.
>
> The other classroom books have very graphic and uncompromising illustrations of sex and genitalia. These were not communicated to parents before students had access to them.
>
> The fourth or eighth grade students are required to share their pronouns. My fifth grader asserted himself as "male and straight" to his teacher after I shared my concerns with her after he came home confused, distressed and asked if he was really born a boy and if he might grow breasts. She

---

75. Rohi's Readery, "Collaborations," *Rohi's Readery*. See Flagler Montessori School, Casa Ranch Montessori.

76. Drag Story Hour NYC, "Events: Program Partners," *Drag Story Hour NYC*. See Greenpoint Montessori School, Brooklyn Heights Montessori School.

77. Sex transitioning is pushed because of gender dysphoria, a psychological disorder where a person feels he or she is of the opposite sex.

continued to confuse him (11 years old), telling him, "There are many kinds of straight."

He was also told that anyone can have a period. The children were divided by "people who have periods" and "people who don't" for health reasons.

Children were consistently redirected by adults after saying things like, "Let's go boys!" to their classmates at recess because "boys" is not inclusive.

My second grader's teacher gave gender identity lessons to small groups followed by a story that reads as a 10-year-old's transgender memoir, *George*, a book intended for middle schoolers. She read this book to a mixed age class of 6 to 8-year-olds. This book extensively discusses the use of medication and surgery to change your body to a different sex, pornography, body dysphoria, hiding web browser history from parents, feeling good wearing a friend's silky underwear and more.

I wouldn't be surprised if drag queen story hour is coming to the school next.

If we hadn't experienced all of this firsthand, I wouldn't understand the alarm and heightened concerns regarding this "trend" of sexualizing children. It's all too absurd to believe. I am still in absolute shock of what we went through. I addressed everything along the way with the teachers and lost complete trust in their judgment and abilities. After meeting with school administration and hearing the defenses, we are in the process of making decisions for next year. [78]

It is entirely inappropriate for teachers to be having conversations with students about gender identity, including "picking their gender," ever, even when children are older.[79] Sexual orientation instruction is completely improper. Make no mistake, it is *not* about "the birds and the bees." Instead, children are taught that you can be anything you want to be. Therefore, you can change from a boy to a girl and vice versa, there are more than two genders, you can be addressed any way you desire, and so on. This instruction can and will psychologically harm

---

78. Mad Mom, "Groomer Schools 4: Drag Queen Story Hour," *New Discourses Podcast*, June 27, 2022.

79. Lavietes, Matt, "Florida Gov. Ron DeSantis signals support for 'Don't Say Gay' bill," *NBC News*, February 8, 2022.

children who are just beginning to grasp the facts of reality and now are getting the message that reality not only is unstable, but that they can change their sex at whim. Montessori had something to say about the importance of reality:

> *But how can the imagination of children be developed by what is, on the contrary, the fruit of our imagination? It is we who imagine, not they; they believe, they do not imagine. Credulity is, indeed, a characteristic of immature minds which lack experience and knowledge of realities, and are yet devoid of intelligence which distinguishes the true from the false, the beautiful from the ugly, the possible from the impossible.*[80]
>
> *Education, therefore, should not be directed to credulity but to intelligence. He who bases education on credulity builds upon sand.*[81]
>
> *Is this illusory imagination, based upon credulity, a thing we ought to "develop" in children? We certainly have no wish to see it persist; in fact, we are told that a child "no longer believes in fairy-tales," we rejoice. We say then: "He is no longer a baby." This is what should happen and we await it: the day will come when he will no longer believe these stories.*[82]
>
> *The child overcomes his difficulties in spite of our endeavor to keep him in ignorance and illusion. The child overcomes himself and us. He goes where his internal force of development and maturation lead him. He might, however, say to us: "How much you have made us suffer! The work of raising ourselves was hard enough already, and you oppressed us."*[83]
>
> *The first thing to do is to enrich his life by an environment in which he will become the owner of something, and to enrich his mind by knowledge and experience based on reality.*[84]

Montessori also had something to say about protecting children from psychological harm:

---

80. Maria Montessori, *Spontaneous Activity in Education*, (Robert Bentley) 259.
81. Maria Montessori, *Spontaneous Activity in Education*, (Robert Bentley) 260.
82. Maria Montessori, *Spontaneous Activity in Education*, (Robert Bentley) 262.
83. Ibid.
84. Maria Montessori, *Spontaneous Activity in Education*, (Robert Bentley) 264.

... the child's growth ... should be a matter for scientific care and attention ... Something more is needed than mere physical hygiene. Just as the latter wards off injuries to his body, so we need mental hygiene to protect his mind and soul from harm." [85]

When Florida's legislature passed a bill in 2022 that forbade sexual instruction to children pre-K through third grade, [86] such as instruction on sexual orientation and gender identity, there was an uproar. Opponents criticized the bill by saying that it marginalizes LGBTQ people. Amit Paley, CEO and executive director of The Trevor Project [suicide prevention and crisis intervention organization for LGBTQ+ young people], said, "Lawmakers should be supporting LGBTQ students and their families and encouraging schools to be inclusive, not pitting parents against teachers and erasing the LGBTQ community from public education." [87] Activists say this law implies that students should be ashamed of their sexual orientation and suppress it.

The criticisms of the bill were unconvincing. How can a five-year-old child feel shame over his sexual orientation when he is too young to have a strong sexual attraction for someone he loves? He isn't even close to puberty! In addition, the statement that this law marginalizes LGBTQ people is a weak argument. Who is being marginalized? It can't be the children who are not developed enough psychologically or physiologically to really understand the topic. Apparently, it must be the 'feelings' of the adults in the LGBTQ community.

Being left out happens to almost everyone at some time in their life for various reasons such as: religion, atheism, disagreements, behavior issues, and philosophical positions to name a few. Part of growing up is learning how to deal with it. Mature people do not whine and demand that the rest of the world revolves around them. They learn how to navigate the world through the use of reason. Paley, however, thinks that LGBTQ people are "erased" because they aren't allowed to talk about their sexuality with young children who have no knowledge of sex or

---

85. Maria Montessori, *The Absorbent Mind*, (Dell) 15.
86. "CBS News, "Florida Governor DeSantis defends controversial bill," *CBS News*, March 5, 2022.
Anthony Izaguirre, "Florida Legislature passes 'Don't Say Gay' bill," *Boston Globe*, March 8, 2022.
87. Kiara Alfonseca, "Florida House passes controversial 'Don't Say Gay' bill," *ABC News*, February 24, 2022.

of its role in human life. Since when are teachers and other instructors allowed to talk to children about their sex lives? When I was growing up, adults who did that were considered to be predators. Sex is intensely personal and mature adults do not talk to children, or anyone else for that matter, about their sexual relationships with their partners.[88]

Contradictions that adults accept and even promote confuse a child and make him feel inadequate to learn. When his parents tell him that private body parts are personal and not to be touched by strangers, what is he to think when he is in the process of being sexualized? When strange adults expose themselves to him? When books are read to him that show explicit sex acts? When he is taught how to masturbate? Is it okay to let strangers touch him then?

Gender Transition[89]

Supporting the attempt to transition to the opposite sex during childhood (as was being done at the Montessori school in Minnesota in the previous section) is pure unadulterated evil. Puberty blockers are extremely dangerous. Queer activists claim that puberty blockers merely delay the onset of puberty, but that is not true; they block puberty altogether and, in the process, cause severe injury. The risks for boys who take them are: blood clots, heart problems, high levels of triglycerides in the blood, high levels of potassium in the blood, infertility, high blood pressure, type 2 diabetes, and stroke. The risks for girls are: male pattern baldness, sleep apnea, elevated cholesterol levels, heart problems, high blood pressure, polycythemia (too many red blood cells), blood clots, infertility, drying and thinning of the lining of the vagina, pelvic pain, and discomfort in the clitoris.[90]

According to the FDA, puberty blockers can lead to increased pressure in the skull. The Mayo Clinic reports that this pressure mimics that of a brain tumor and can lead to vision loss.[91] Puberty blockers have also been linked to permanent bone loss. A child, 15 years of age, developed osteoporosis after 15 months of puberty blockers.[92]

---

88. The only exception to this would be talking to your doctor about a problem.
89. Charlotte Cushman, "Yes, Transgender Transformation is Child Abuse," *American Thinker*, June 16, 2022.
90. Logan Lancing, *The Queering of the American Child*, 180.
91. Logan Lancing, *The Queering of the American Child*, 179.
92. Ibid.

The effect suppressing puberty will have on brain development is unknown, an aspect that should be determined before treatment. The brain is crucial to human life—what if the growth of the brain is stunted? There are reasons to suspect that brain development is at risk. Scientists at the University of Glasgow gave sheep some puberty-suppressing treatments and found that the spatial memory of male sheep was damaged.[93]

Christopher Rufo, author of New York Times best-selling book, *America's Cultural Revolution*, asked a physician, in a major children's hospital, who has witnessed how the medical field has embraced transgender ideology, for his opinion on the future of transgender medicine. He answered in anonymity:

> I don't know. I pray there is a change. One of the things I've been thinking about is what puberty blockers do to children. This medication is called a "gonadotropin releasing hormone agonist" and it comes in the form of monthly injections or an implant. And because it simulates the activity of this hormone, it shuts down the activity of the hypothalamus. The hypothalamus is this almond-sized structure in your brain, it's one of the most primal structures we have, and it controls all the other hormonal structures in your body – your sexual development, your emotions, your fight-or-flight response, everything. But it shouldn't be described in such cold physiological terms because your hypothalamus is not just a hormone factory. It's this system that allows you to stand in awe of the beauty of a sunset, or to hear the sounds of orchestral music and to stop whatever you're doing and want to listen. And I always think that if someone were to ask me, where is it that you would look for the divine spark in each individual? I would say that it would be somewhere "beneath the inner chamber," which is the Greek derivation of the term hypothalamus. To shut down that system is to shut down what makes us human.[94]

It has been claimed that a person's sex can be changed because it isn't set at birth—it's "assigned" at birth. Dr. Mariam Grossman, a board-certified child and adolescent psychiatrist, who has been treating patients for forty-five years, stresses, "Sex is not assigned at birth, sex is *established* at conception and it is recognized at birth, if not earlier."[95]

---

93. Logan Lancing, *The Queering of the American Child*, 179.
94. Logan Lancing, *The Queering of the American Child*, 191–192.
95. Mariam Grossman testifies to US House Committee, "She Destroys Gender Ideology

A person can't change his sex. We are all born with male or female chromosomes (absent rare genetic anomalies) that exist in every cell of our bodies, and that doesn't change by taking hormones or by adding or subtracting body parts. It is psychologically damaging to spit at reality by pretending to be something you are not. Surgically altering one's body is not only gruesome and horrific, it is also irreversible. It is beyond tragic that there are children who wish to change to the opposite sex because they "feel" like the opposite sex, want to be accepted, or want to escape condemnation for being white.[96] Anyone promoting this mutilation procedure for children should be ashamed of himself.

How is permanently altering a child's body based on the child's "feelings" not child abuse? So, if a child "feels" like jumping off a cliff, do we let him? What if he "feels" like cutting off his fingers? Do we let him do that? What if the child feels, not merely pretends to be, but feels, like a furry? (More about furries in the next section.) Do we allow him to use a litter box or to hiss at a classmate? Do we allow him to ignore reality? Or do we help him to face reality? And when we don't help him, when we actually aid him in placing his feelings above reality, such as damaging his body, how does that not result in serious physical or emotional harm? Especially a few years later or during adulthood, when he hates and resents what was done to him?[97]

> *His mentality differs from ours; … and loves to wander in the fascinating worlds of unreality, a tendency which is also characteristic of savage peoples.*[98]
>
> …
>
> *Instead of indulging in such flights of scientific fancy as these, it would be much simpler to declare that an organism as yet immature, like that of the child, has remote affinities with mentalities less mature than our own, like those of savages. But even if we refrain from interfering with the belief of those who interpret childish mentality as "a savage state," we may point out that as, in any case, this savage state is transient, and must be superseded, education should help the child to overcome it; it should not develop the savage state, nor keep the child therein.*[99]

---

in 5 Minutes," *YouTube*, August 10, 2023.

96. Lisa Littman, "Parent reports of adolescents," *Plos/One* 14, no 3 (August 2018).

97. Thomas D. Steensma, Ph.D., et al, "Factors Associated With Desistence and Persistence," *Journal of the American Academy of Child & Adolescent Psychiatry* 52, no. 6 (June 2013).

98. Maria Montessori, *Spontaneous Activity in Education*, (Robert Bentley) 255.

99. Ibid.

...

What is it that is thus being cultivated in these immature minds? What do we find akin to this in the adult world which will enable us to understand for what definitive forms we prepare the mind by such a method of education? There are, indeed, men who really take a tree for a throne, and issue royal commands: some believe themselves to be God, for "false perceptions," or the graver form, "illusions," are the beginning of false reasoning, and the concomitants of delirium. The insane produce nothing, nor can those children, condemned to the immobility of an education which tends to develop their innocent manifestations of unsatisfied desires into mania, produce anything either for themselves or others. We, however, suppose that we are developing the imagination of children by making them accept fantastic things as realities.[100]

The parents who allow their child to physically alter his body to give the superficial, unconvincing costume of the opposite sex are teaching their child that his whims are above reality. Teachers who tell children that they can change their sex are doing the same thing. Furthermore, a teacher is not the child's doctor and has no business telling him that he can change his sex. Schools are not medical institutions and talks of this nature are completely out of line.

When a child says he feels like the opposite sex, the reason adults do not tell him that feelings are not facts is because, thanks to progressive education, they think there is no such thing as objective reality and that adults are not the authority—the child's feelings are! So, how can parents say no to a child who "knows his own truth?"

The ultimate consequences will be children who grow up and carry on with a demented view of reality. They will be mutilated adults who have been robbed of their own natural bodies when they were innocent and trusting children. They will be robbed of puberty, a time in their lives when children mature in body and mind. As adults, they will have been robbed of the ability to produce children without unnatural, man-made complications. Any child who goes on puberty blockers has effectively been sterilized. There is more than just the physical irreversible damage. Puberty is when you reach both sexual and mental maturity. The lack of self-autonomy will create psychological and emotional harm.[101] How?

---

100. Maria Montessori, *Spontaneous Activity in Education*, (Robert Bentley) 258–259.
101. Lancer, Darlene, "Exploring Autonomy, Locus of Control, and Self-Efficacy,"

By telling a child he can be the opposite sex, by breezily declaring he can "identify" however he wants, the adult is really telling him that reality can be anything he wants, that reality is fluid, that A is not A. The spoon he drops may not hit the floor every time if he just wishes hard enough. The ultimate in denying reality is sex change—"gender transition." Indulging children with "transgender affirmations" is a firm attack on truth allowed by pathetically weak parents and teachers. It is child abuse, brutal child abuse, and, if not stopped, children and our culture will suffer terribly for it.

Furries [102]

The rejection of reality leads to another extreme form of claiming to

---

PsychCentral, May 17, 2016.

102. Libs of TikTok (@libsoftiktok), "BREAKING: Photos have surfaced," *X.com*, April 17, 2024.

Jones, Alex (@RealAlexJones)," Private Investigator Exposes," *X.com*, August 9, 2024.

Raichik, Chaya (@ChayaRaichik10), "Guys there's no evidence of furries," *X.com*, April 18.

Libs of TikTok (@libsoftiktok), "Rep. Charise Davids (D-KS) attended and promoted," *X.com*, June 24, 2024.

End Wokeness (@EndWokenes), "What a time to be alive," *X.com*, April 18, 2024.

End Wokeness (@EndWokenes), "LEGO just released a LGBTQ+ Pride video," *X.com*, June 20, 2024.

E (@ElijahSchaffer), "INSANE: Furries take over a public school," *X.com*, April 19, 2024.

Libs of TikTok (@libsoftiktok), "The media is going all out to cover up for the furries," *X.com*, April 18, 2024.

Gays Against Groomers (@againstgrmrs), "The furries are out of hand," *X.com*, August 28, 2024.

Savage, Michael (@ASavageNation), "A Child Thinks he is a Furry Animal," *X.com*, July 8, 2023.

Heartland Signal (@HeartlandSignal), "Nebraska State Sen. Bostelman (R) falsely says," *X.com*, March 28, 2022.

Off Topic Show (@OffTopicShow2), "From Pipes to Litter Boxes," *X.com*, June 7, 2024.

Kaczynki, Andy (@KFILE), "At an event last week, the GOP," *X.com*, October 3, 2022.

Sullivan, Sharon, "'They Are Putting Litter Boxes in Schools'," *Colorado Times Recorder*, October 4, 2022.

being born in the wrong body—furries. The definition is explained in encyclopedia.com:

> The word *furries* is an identity-based term that is embraced by people who enjoy anthropomorphic (animals endowed with human traits) art, online animal role-playing, and/or dressing up in cartoon animal costumes. The furry subculture is a well-organized and wide-ranging phenomenon that cohered in the early 1980s in the United States. All furries have an interest in anthropomorphics which may manifest itself as a hobby or as a central aspect of lifestyle and identity. For instance, some furries simply may have a strong interest in cartoon animals and comics, whereas others integrate their animal-focused interests into their erotic life.
>
> Furries have their own animal-focused art, conferences, and language. Sometimes called Furspeak, the vocabulary is a mixture of technological terms, puns, and onomatopoeic words that classify furry activities, feelings, and personalities. "Fursuiters" are furries who don full-body animal costumes that reflect an individual's "inner animal" or speak more broadly to the spiritual bond a furry shares with a specific animal. Foxes, bears, lions, cats, and tigers are popular personal "totems" adopted by furries. "Scritching" is an act of scratching or cuddling between furries that shows affection but also may function as a "mating call" or provide evidence that a furry is feeling "yiffy," or ready for sex. "Furverts" are people who are sexually attracted to mascots and others dressed up in furry costumes. Online activity takes place in furry MUCKs (multi-user chat kingdoms) where furries invent characters ("fursonas") and live out their sexual and anthropomorphic fantasies in virtual space. "Plushophiles," or "plushies," are furries who feel an erotic attraction to stuffed animals and may engage in sexual activity with their collections.[103]

Some children in public schools are now identifying as furries, and the adults in authority around them too often allow it. The children act like furries, dress in furry costumes, use furspeak, and even go so far as to ask to use a litter box. I even know of a child taken for a doctor appointment who communicated by growling. There are reports of students in school being harassed by furries. In the spring of 2024, some students at Mt. Nebo Middle School in Utah were so upset about being bitten, scratched, barked at, and chased that they walked out of class and held an hour-long protest.[104]

---

103. Gates, Katherine, "Furries," *Deviant Desires: Incredibly Strange Sex*.
104. Trevor Myers, "Students walk out of middle school to protest 'furries,' *ABC.com*,

A furry is not the innocent child temporarily pretending to be a dog or a cat, which is a result of normal childhood imagination. The furry phenomenon is actually a form of queer theory where adults foster abnormality by allowing, and even encouraging, these delusions. The fact of reality is that children cannot be dogs or cats—they can only be human beings. The furry movement is an outright denial of reality.

Queer theory promotes sexual abnormality, but this fact is hidden by the excuse that the child is just pretending to be an animal, and all kids love animals and pretend to be animals. Despite the denials, sexual activity does take place with furries. Another concerning aspect is the sadomasochism that is involved, both with the furry and the person "handler" enabling him to engage in such a critical rejection of who he really is, especially when a collar and leash is put around the neck of the furry.

Fake Pronouns

Addressing children with fake pronouns, in conjunction with adults encouraging transgenderism, confuses children about their bodies. Other children are pressured to endorse this fantasy when addressing their friends, or they are accused of being bullies. Furthermore, plural pronouns eliminate individuality. Linda Goudsmit, author of *Space Is No Longer the Final Frontier–Reality Is*, explains:

> In an information war, fought without bullets or bombs, language is weaponized. The globalist campaign promoting gender fluidity in order to destroy individual selfness, manipulates spoken and written language to achieve its goal. Perversion of pronoun usage in the English language has a particularly destructive political purpose. The enemies of national and individual sovereignty are revising language to reflect human existence without the boundaries of self. Words matter. The switch to third-person plural gender-neutral language is a weapon of mass psychological destruction that begins in early childhood.
>
> Consider this: young children who do not learn the first-and-second person individual and possessive pronouns *I, me, mine, you, yours, he, him, his, she, her, hers* do not learn to name or identify themselves or others as individual gendered selves. Without a personal, individual, gendered, identical self, children become confused, destabilized, and vulnerable.

April 17, 2024.

Instead of singular pronouns, young children are intentionally being taught to use third person plural pronouns they, them, theirs, so that they identify themselves in terms of the non-gendered collective. It is linguistic demolition of the individual. Plural pronouns effectively erase the concept of an individual self from the English language, and support the replacement of the individual with the preferred non-gendered collective identity.[105]

Removing the word "I" is removing the individual, and replacing "I" with plural pronouns is an assault on independence and individualism. It is blatant collectivism consistent with John Dewey and Karl Marx who held that an individual is not self-created, he is created from his social relations.[106] Any acceptance of using plural pronouns and thereby erasing the individual is a direct assault on the Montessori Method.

At first, he was guided by an impersonal force seeming to be hidden within him; now he is guided by his conscious "I," by his own personal self…[107]

… education that represses and rejects the promptings of the moral self, that erects obstacles and barriers in the way of the development of intelligence, that condemns huge sectors of the population to ignorance is a crime.[108]

Pedophilia[109]

It won't be long before they call for kids to be sexually molested to ensure they will have a messed-up sexuality. Pedophilia is next and the street was paved for it years ago.

I do not know of any Montessori educators who are guilty of pedophilia, but I am including the topic in this book, because this is where the Queer Theory movement is headed, and people need to be aware of it to protect their children. Not all homosexuals or lesbians participate in pedophilia, or support the LGBT movement for that matter, but it is a stated goal of the LGBT activists nonetheless.

---

105. Linda Goudsmit, *Space Is No Longer,* 202–203.
106. Wikipedia, "Marx's theory of human nature," *Wikipedia.org,* December 2017.
107. Maria Montessori, *The Absorbent Mind,* (Dell) 167.
108. Maria Montessori, "Preface" in *Education and Peace.*
109. Charlotte Cushman, "After Drag Queens, Pedophilia is Next," *American Thinker,* June 18, 2022.

Once you have cheapened sex, sexualized children, and asserted a child is as sexual as an adult and has his own ability to consent to sex, as Queer theorists do, it is a very short hop to pedophilia. Dennis Altman, for example, an Australian academic and gay rights activist, condones pedophilia in his book *Homosexual Oppression and Liberation*:

> One might also argue that since no one advocates preventing all interaction between children and adults, it is making too much of sex to argue that this relationship alone should be prohibited.
>
> ...
>
> If sexuality were free from the sorts of pressures that exist in our society—it would be utopian to argue for *no* social pressures that exist in our society—I suspect child/adult sex would be fairly common, though not perhaps as common as sex among children themselves.[110]

The most influential LGBT intellectual in history, Michel Foucault, thought it was perfectly fine for a child to consent to sex.[111] Simone de Beauvoir, the most famous feminist in history, once signed a petition defending men who had sex with 13-year-old girls.[112]

In 2015, Gayle S. Rubin promoted pedophilia in her document "Thinking Sex" which was quoted in the Queer Theory section of this book.[113] Ole Martin Moen, a gay professor in Norway who identifies as queer, stated that "the mental state of finding children sexually attractive is very common" and that a "percentage of high school students have an innate pedophilic sexual identity."[114]

Children are not ready for sex, not physically or psychologically. Sex is the ultimate expression of value, of oneself and the other person, and understanding that value only comes about with the ability to reason which children haven't fully developed. As Ronald Pisaturo said to me, "Child sexuality is wrong because children don't have the reasoning ability to deal with sex. But if sexuality is mindless, as LGBT ideology holds, then children do have the ability to deal with sex."[115]

---

110. Ronald Pisaturo, *Masculine Power, Feminine Beauty*.
111. Michel Foucault, "The Danger of Child Sexuality," April 4, 1978.
112. Marie Doezema, "France, Where Age of Consent Is Up for Debate," *The Atlantic*, March 10, 2008.
113. Gayle Rubin, "Chapter 9 Thinking Sex," *Culture Society and Sexuality*.
114. Joshua Young, "Norway Ethics professor calls for normalization of pedophilia," *The Post Millennial*, June 11, 2022.
115. Ronald Pisaturo, *Masculine Power, Feminine Beauty*.

Sex is not to be degraded. It is not like the self-loathing that drag queens portray. Any adult who believes that sexuality is mindless is also not ready for sex.

The advocates of social justice must destroy the culture to destroy capitalism and freedom. Destroying the minds of innocent children by degrading the sacred act of sex is one of their enabling goals. Their next step is pedophilia. They have come right out and promoted it, and it has to be taken seriously because they mean it.

Restorative Justice

Restorative justice is a movement, rooted in social justice, that seeks to replace our existing systems of punitive justice with a social system of control. Punitive measures, such as removing criminals from society, are considered to be ineffective, so the goal is to control crime more successfully by helping victims heal from their trauma and by fostering genuine accountability in criminals and reintegrating them into society.

Schools that institute restorative justice programs often do not discipline children who initiate aggression against others. Instead, the aggressor and the victim have conversations to understand how the victim was harmed and how to repair the damage, and why the transgressor committed the transgression. Repeat offenders are not punished or suspended, and a paper trail is not established of their misbehaviors. During their "conversations," bystanders may also participate. That can include the entire class and often takes a lot of time away from class time learning. Restorative justice has been implemented in Montessori schools in Minnesota,[116] Florida,[117] Connecticut,[118] Washington,[119] New Jersey,[120] and Washington, D.C.[121]

---

116. Great River School, "January 2022 GRS Board Updates," *GreatRiverSchool.org*, February 2, 2022.

Saint Paul Federation of Educators, "Restorative Practices," *SPFE28.org*, Minnesota.

117. Innovation Montessori, "Fast Facts," *innovationmontessori.com*. Florida, Restorative Justice Information.

118. Christian Robles, "Closing School Climate Gaps," *Yale College Education Studies Program*, Spring 2023. Connecticut.

119. Montessori Country School, "Conflict Resolution Models used," *Montessori Country School*. Washington.

120. Edgemont Montessori School, "Restorative Justice," *Edgemont Montessori School*, 2024. New Jersey.

121. My School DC, "Lee Montessori PCS – Brookland," *My School DC*. Washington,

While effective communication is important, good behavior in the Montessori classroom is not reliant upon conversations. As was explained earlier, good behavior is attained when a child achieves self-discipline through normalization.

> *Normalization comes about through "concentration" on a piece of work.*[122]

When a child enters a Montessori school at age two and a half to three years of age, he usually lacks focus and body control, and he may flit around the room interrupting the other children. Some go from activity to activity rarely completing any of them, showing a lack of concentration. This can go on for days or months or even years, but once he finds an activity that captures his interest, he learns to concentrate using his will, and those deviations eventually disappear. Montessori was ecstatic to discover the true nature of the child.

> *I watched them, seeking to understand the secret of these souls, of whose greatness I had been so ignorant! As I stood in meditation among the eager children, the discovery that it was knowledge they loved…filled me with wonder and made me think of the greatness of the human soul!*[123]

Until the child reaches normalization, the teacher must discipline him, sometimes regularly, and Montessori thought that misbehavior should be handled with firmness.

> *When the teachers were weary of my observations, they began to allow the children to do whatever they pleased. I saw children with their feet on the tables, or fingers in their noses, and no intervention was made to correct them. I saw others push their companions, and I saw on the faces of these an expression of violence, and not the slightest attention on the part of the teacher. Then I had to intervene to show with what absolute rigor it is necessary to hinder, and little by little suppress, all those things which we must not do so that the child may come to discern clearly between good and evil.*[124]

D.C.
    122. Maria Montessori, *The Absorbent Mind*, (Dell) 206.
    123. Maria Montessori, The *Montessori Method*, (Schocken) 300.
    124. Maria Montessori, The *Montessori Method*, (Schocken) 92–93.

In her original schools, consequences were used, one of which was intervention.

> *If at this stage there is some child who persistently annoys the others, the most practical thing to do is interrupt him. It is true that we have said and repeated often enough, that when a child is absorbed in his work, one must refrain from interfering.... [N]evertheless, the right technique now is just the opposite; it is to break the flow of the disturbing activity....*[125]

Another discipline technique was used in Montessori's original schools with success—time-outs. A time-out is "a brief suspension of activity: break; a quiet period used especially as a disciplinary measure for children."[126] Time-outs can be used to calm a child or to stop an unacceptable behavior. E. M. Standing, author of *Maria Montessori: Her Life and Work*, recalls:

> I once sent a questionnaire round to a number of long-established Montessori schools, and one of the questions in it was this: What use do you make of punishments? One directress wrote: "Work is its own reward. Punishments are rare; a troublesome child might be removed from her companions until she is ready to behave properly." Another said: "With younger children the greatest reward is to be able to pass on to a new stage in each subject. It is a punishment to a child not to be able to use the apparatus, but to sit still and do nothing." Another teacher (with twenty years of experience behind her) said: "If a warning does not suffice, the offender is separated from other children and made to sit beside the directress.[127] The lessons given by the directress to other children generally arouse interest and the child settles down to work. Either this or she becomes bored and returns to her place. This 'punishment' proves quite sufficient."[128]

Montessori wrote more fully about isolating a child:

> *As far as punishments are concerned, we frequently found ourselves confronted with children who disturbed others, but who would not*

---

125. Maria Montessori, *The Absorbent Mind*, (Dell) 278–279.
126. Merriam-Webster Dictionary, "time-out," *Merriam-Webster Dictionary*.
127. Even though the child is sitting next to an adult, this is still a time-out by definition.
128. E. M. Standing, *Maria Montessori: Her Life and Work*, 44.

> listen to our entreaties. We immediately had them examined by a physician, but very often they turned out to be normal. We then placed a little table in a corner of the room and, thereby isolating the child, we made him sit in an armchair where he could be seen by his companions and gave him all the objects he desires. This isolation always succeeded in calming the child. From his position he could see all of his companions, and their way of acting was an object lesson in behavior more effective than words of his teacher could have been. Little by little he came to realize the advantages of being with the others and to desire to act as they did. In this way we imparted discipline to all the children who at first had seemed to us to be rebels... I do not know what happened within the souls of the isolated children, but certainly their conversions were always true and lasting. They became proud of their work and behavior, and they generally retained a tender affection for their teacher and for me. [129]

Instead of giving the child more work to punish misbehavior, she advocated withdrawing him from work and putting him in a position where he could learn proper behavior by observing the rest of the children. He also could observe the work all around him and see what he was missing. This was very effective. Isolation coupled with observation resulted in the misbehaving child discovering interesting work.

Montessori put the responsibility of a well-run class directly upon the teacher.

> [W]hen her class becomes undisciplined, the teacher sees in the disorder merely an indication of some error that she has made; she seeks this out and corrects it. [130]

Effective communication works very well with some children and in some situations, but one must understand that it is not a one-size-fits-all solution. Montessori understood that the teacher needs to evaluate each situation and treat the children accordingly, often with a consequence. Does the insolent, lippy child need a time-out? Should she separate the violent repeat offender from the other children? Maybe the impulsive child needs to practice moving slower. The attention seeker needs to try again without interrupting others. Another child needs to write an

---
129. Maria Montessori, *The Discovery of the Child*, 86.
130. Maria Montessori, *The Absorbent Mind*, (Dell) 285.

essay explaining why what he did was wrong and how he can improve his behavior next time. Or maybe the teacher needs to give an impolite child some grace and courtesy lessons.

If she is faced with a class of unruly children, she needs to be assertive and stop any negative activity. Montessori thought that useless or dangerous acts *"must be suppressed, destroyed."* [131] The teacher should determine how that should be done, which will depend on the circumstances, and then do it with no hesitation:

> *When called on to direct a class of such children, the teacher may find herself in an agonizing situation if she is armed with no other weapon than the basic idea of offering the means of development and of letting them express themselves freely. The little hell that has begun to break loose in these children will drag to itself everything within reach, and the teacher, if she remains passive, will be overwhelmed by confusion and an almost unbelievable noise... She must call to them, wake them up, by her voice and thought. A vigorous and firm call is the only true act of kindness toward these little minds. Do not fear to destroy evil; it is only good that we must fear to destroy. Just as we must call a child's name before he can answer, so we must call the soul vigorously if we wish to awaken it. The teacher must remove her apparatus from the school and take away the principles from what she has learned; then she must face this question of the call, practically and alone. Only her intelligence can solve the problem, which will be different in every case. The teacher knows the fundamental symptoms and the certain remedies; she knows the theory of the treatment. All the rest depends on her...It is for her to judge whether it is better for her to raise her voice amid the general hubbub, or to whisper to a few children, so that the others become curious to hear, and peace is restored again.*
>
> *A teacher of experience never has grave disorder in her class because, before she draws aside to leave the children free, she watches and directs them for some time, preparing them in a negative sense, that is to say, by eliminating their uncontrolled movements.* [132]

The children in Montessori's schools were permitted to work toward the ultimate goal of self-discipline by working with materials that gave

---

131. Maria Montessori, The *Montessori Method*, (Schocken) 88.
132. Maria Montessori, *The Absorbent Mind*, (Dell) 268–269.

them an understanding of the facts of reality. This process of developing self-discipline was managed by the teacher. The children were permitted to work without restrictions as long as they were engaged in purposeful activity, but if the behavior of any of the children became detrimental to themselves or someone else, the teacher was responsible for taking appropriate action. Montessori's method of discipline was groundbreaking because the children were not disciplined for the purpose of obedience to the teacher, as was traditionally done. Instead, they were disciplined for the purpose of developing independence.

One problem with the restorative justice approach is that peace reconciliation only works with people who want reconciliation. It doesn't work with those who want to continue their misbehavior. The restorative justice approach is unfair to an innocent victim who has been attacked repeatedly by the same aggressor, and it even provides an opportunity for the aggressor to continue to attack the victim by making the victim accept the attacks. A talk won't work here. The aggressor needs consequences and the victim needs protection. Even if the participants want peace, understanding a long, complicated discussion can be very difficult for children who are still learning how to reason. Rules and the purposes of rules and the ramifications of breaking them always need to be explained to children, but one must understand that they do not have an adult understanding of those rules yet, and so brevity and directness help make them clear.

Another problem with the restorative justice approach is that it can take up too much time during class time. The purpose of school is to learn, not to spend inordinate amounts of time trying to solve social problems. Communication and understanding others are important, but they shouldn't take day after day after day. The job of the teacher is to educate children; she is not their therapist. If a child has a habit of interfering with the work of his classmates and communication didn't work, the teacher needs to stop him, separate him, and move on. No child should be allowed to abuse the rights of others and disrupt the class. If the child does not respond to appropriate disciplinary procedures, he needs additional help, and he needs to get it outside of school with trusted professionals.[133]

Restorative justice depends on social interaction to solve behavior difficulties rather than a reality-based approach such as the perpetrator

---

133. The place to start is with the child's pediatrician to rule out any physical ailments.

experiencing consequences for his actions. Without consequences, he doesn't learn logic, rules, or boundaries. During the talks with the victim and his classmates, he becomes reliant upon what others say about his or someone else's behavior instead of reality itself. He can also lie about why he misbehaved if he isn't honest. Seeking a socially based solution creates confusion in the minds of children and ultimately makes them, both victim and aggressor, dependent on others for their self-image.

Social justice, restorative justice, Marxism, and LGBT are all collectivist ideologies that are anti-Montessori. Rather than treating children as individuals and considering the context of the problem, they advocate the same solutions for everyone. They all pontificate about the "oppressed," yet when one child repeatedly initiates violent aggressions, the victim is the one who is truly oppressed. Rather than letting the aggressor know in no uncertain terms that it is wrong to initiate violence, the social justice collectivist groups support a system that puts the oppressor and the oppressed on the same moral level by having a "talk" without a consequence for the aggressor. This approach does not give children a clear idea of the difference between right and wrong. The Montessori approach does teach the difference by using confrontation, consequences, and ultimately the opportunity for normalization.

Revisionist History

Throughout history when communists/socialists/fascists are preparing to take over a country, they create an educational system that keeps the population uneducated, weak, and unstable. They hide the fact that they are teaching incorrect history, changing it, or even eliminating it altogether. They also wipe out that country's culture by eliminating traditions such as Halloween and Christmas. Their goal is for citizens to engage in hatred—self-hatred. A self-hating culture is a meek culture prepped for any totalitarian to take over.

There are Montessorians who are cooperating with these attempts to erase our history and culture such as eliminating the stories of Thanksgiving and Columbus. In view of that, I have included some articles in the appendix about Columbus, the Pilgrims, and Pocahontas.

A study of the history and culture of one's own country is a vital element of education. It is important for children to understand why they are living the way they are, and that it is a result of what people who lived before them did. They need to be able to connect the dots—these prevailing thoughts led to fights, these ideas led to prosperity, this action led to that one, and so on. Making these kinds of connections strengthens the child's ability to think logically.

It is sad and frightening that multiculturalism has made headway in education.[134] Multiculturalism holds that all cultures, whether they value life or not, are equal in value. According to multiculturalism, the primary unit of society is the group. It holds, therefore, that all groups and cultures are to be treated equally in all respects. It is considered virtuous to study other cultures, but not the culture of the United States. America, the nation founded on the principle of individual rights, is accused of being repressive. According to multiculturalism, all cultures are equal in value except western cultures, which are deemed more aggressive, violent and immoral.

It is very damaging to allow an educational environment where children celebrate everybody else's culture or history, but not their own. The American child, who is denied knowledge about his culture, is given the message that he is either oppressed or the oppressor because of his race, sex, family, culture, or country. The real oppressors are the Marxists who want to enslave the people through communism.

The Family

One of the forty-five goals read into the Congressional Record for a communist takeover of the United States was to discredit the family and to "emphasize the need to raise children away from the negative influence of parents." As we learned from the Drag Pedagogy paper, one of their goals is to extinguish the traditional family by grooming children to join the family of queers. This is because Marxists think that parents who want to keep their children racially and sexually innocent pose a threat to the Marxist plan to destabilize society. Therefore, the family unit must be destroyed. Any school that includes drag or queer pedagogy in its classroom contributes to this goal.

When teachers hide from parents certain topics that are being taught to their child or information about the child's development, such as his desire to transition to the opposite sex, or even tell the child not to tell

---

134. Robert Holland and Don Soifer, "Radical multiculturalism a growing problem in public schools," *The Daily Caller*, September 16, 2010.

their parents what is going on, those teachers are crossing a forbidden line. Teachers are not the parents of their students and have no right whatsoever to conceal such information. Parents have the sole right to know what is taught to their child. They bore that child, they support that child, and they are responsible for that child. The teacher may not encroach upon that right, and if she does, she is standing between the child and his parents, and, hence, undermining the family. Montessori supported the traditional family.

> *There is a voluntary fundamental quality upon which not only are the superficial relations between man and man based, but on which the very edifice of society is erected. This quality is known as "continuity." The social structure is founded upon the fact that men can work steadily and produce within certain average limits on which the economic equilibrium of a people is constructed. The social relations which are the basis of the reproduction of the species are founded upon the continuous union of parents in marriage. The family and productive work: these are the two pivots of society; they rest upon the greatest volitive quality: constancy, or persistence.*[135]

Engels thought that the family was a result of capitalism. During the early stages of human evolution, everyone belonged to the community, and property was owned and shared collectively. With the creation of wealth and private property, people wanted to be able to pass it on to their own children. In the collective community, there was no limitation to sexual access, so the paternity and their correct heirs were difficult to ascertain. With families, there was no question as to who the heirs were. Marxists thought that families perpetuated capitalism by passing on wealth, which created inequality. Therefore, as stated in *The Communist Manifesto*, one of the goals of socialism/communism is to dismantle the family.

> Abolition (*Aufhebung*) of the family! Even the most radical flare up at this infamous proposal of the Communists.

> On what foundation is the present family, the bourgeois family, based? On capital, on private gain. In its completely developed form, this family exists only among the bourgeoisie. But this state of things finds its

---
135. Maria Montessori, *Spontaneous Activity in Education*, (Robert Bentley) 178.

> complement in the practical absence of the family among the proletarians, and in public prostitution.
>
> The bourgeois family will vanish as a matter of course when its complement vanishes, and both will vanish with the vanishing of capital.
>
> Do you charge us with wanting to stop the exploitation of children by their parents? To this crime we plead guilty.
>
> But, you say, we destroy the most hallowed of relations when we replace home education by social.[136]

Today the family has evolved to mean a whole lot more than just passing on inheritance. People now pursue their happiness by trying to find someone to love and with whom they can create a happy family. This makes it even worse for Marxists because totalitarian regimes demand that the individual live for the State, not for himself, and families just get in the way. As Benito Mussolini said, "Everything in the State, nothing outside the State, nothing against the State."[137] Statists want to destroy a country's culture to extinguish the independence of its citizens. They do that by trying to stop them from pursuing values, because when individuals seek out close relationships, they are not focused on sacrificing for the State.

The argument that marriage and family are not good institutions because some or even many don't work out, is invalid. All families are different, just like all marriages are different, and all relationships are different. Some are good, some bad, and some in between. But some bad marriages or bad families don't mean those institutions as such are not worth pursuing. Most people want to be happy and they want their close relationships to work out. They want people to be close to, and want to live with people that they care about and that care about them. (However, the family is not more important than the individual and a grown child does not owe allegiance, no matter what, to his family, especially when their values clash with his in a way that he cannot tolerate such as immoral behavior.)

Almost every family has problems or challenges at some time or an-

---

136. Karl Marx and Friedrich Engels, "Manifesto of the Communist Party," *Internet Archive*, 1848.

137. Villa La Pietra, NYU, Florence, "Everything Within the State," *Villa La Pietra*, November 3, 2015.

other, such as black sheep, stressful relationships, harsh disagreements, and so on. Some problems are serious and some are minor. But as horrible as some families are, it is far preferable for a child to be raised in a family, than to be raised by the State. At least if a child has a bad upbringing, he can choose to leave his family when he comes of age. But if he is raised by the State, how can he escape it? And at least with a family, the child has a chance at being loved and cherished, but would never have that with the State. Furthermore, families actually promote independence from government. When you have people to lean on, to support you, you don't need a government "safety net" with obedience strings attached. The state "family" is a con. The State wants work slaves to fund their power. History shows that a subjugated people are definitely not treated "like family."

The institution of "family" is constantly evolving. People often try to avoid the mistakes their parents made. I observed a family with a relative who had a mental delay and was treated like dirt by his immediate family. The next generation recognized how unfair and cruel that was and always treated him with respect. Next generations can identify contradictions and irrationalities and choose to avoid them. The growth of knowledge and the use of reason can only have a positive effect on this process, and I think, families will get better and stronger because of it.

While marriage and family are valid institutions, not everyone chooses to marry and create a family, and that's fine. However, it doesn't take away from the fact that families are a legitimate value for a great many people. Destroying rational values is the repudiation of morality, and the result is emotional despair. When rational values are pursued and achieved, the result is an emotional state of happiness. Raising a child and watching him grow into an independent, happy individual is one of the greatest joys in life. The family needs to be preserved whether everyone chooses to have one or not.

CHAPTER 3
Montessori Organizations That Promote Social Justice

In this chapter you will learn about four major Montessori organizations (and some schools) that have been promoting and participating in social justice: Association Montessori International, American Montessori Society, National Center for Montessori in the Public Sector, and Montessori for Social Justice. As a reminder of what I said in the introduction, not every Montessori school is participating in implementing social justice, but it is the trend, and as we've seen with other institutions, it will spread if people do not identify it and reject it.

Association Montessori International (AMI)

Association Montessori International (AMI) was founded in 1929 in the Netherlands by Maria Montessori to train teachers to implement the Montessori Method of education and safeguard the integrity of the method after her death.[1] Association Montessori International/United States of America (AMI/USA) is an affiliate of AMI.

AMI/USA had a refresher course in 2018. The opening speech was given by Gretchen Hall, AMI/USA Board President, who said, "We must stand beside all those who work for social justice on behalf of children. That is our legacy and our mission."[2]

My response: The original mission of AMI was to protect the integrity of Montessori's educational method. In the words of Montessori,

Let us leave the life free to develop within the limits of the good, and let us observe this inner life developing. This is the whole of our mission.[3]

---

1. E. M. Standing, *Maria Montessori Her Life and Work*, 72.
2. AMI/USA, "Keynote Address from Gretchen Hall," *AMI/USA*, February 20, 2018.
3. Deb Chitwood, "Best Maria Montessori Quotes," *Bits of* Positivity (blog), January 10, 2017. See the quote by Maria Montessori, *Dr. Montessori's Own Handbook*.

At this refresher course, there was a workshop entitled "Embracing Equity." The description read:

> Peace education and social justice are cornerstones of the Montessori Philosophy. For adults to effectively talk with children about race and prejudice, we need to explore our own biases and beliefs... Participants will personally reflect in a 'spiritual preparation of self' to confront socialized and entrenched notions of privilege, identity, and social justice.[4]

My response: Peace is a result of a proper education. Montessori education is not about filling the child's mind with race and prejudice. The accurate use of the Montessori method is all about the normalization of the child, respecting the child and treating him as a human with rights. And since the child creates the adult he will become, and adults are responsible for creating and maintaining a civilized society, peace will have a better chance. One can see the results of normalized children in authentic Montessori classrooms—peace. Hence, Montessori concluded that the means to world peace was through education by providing a prepared environment where children can normalize—one of her major points.

> *... children construct their own character, building up in themselves the qualities we admire. These do not spring from our example or admonishments, but they result solely from a long and slow sequence of activities carried out by the child himself between the ages of three and six.*[5]

> *Such experience is not just play, or a series of random activities, but it is work that he has to do in order to grow up.*[6]

> *Directing our action toward mankind means, first and foremost, doing so with regard to the child. The child, that 'forgotten citizen', must be appreciated in accordance with his true value. His rights as a human being who shapes all of mankind must become sacred, and the secret laws of his normal psychic development must light the way for civilization.*[7]

---

4. AMI/USA, "Refresher Course Workshops," AMI/USA, September 12, 2017.
5. Maria Montessori, *The Absorbent Mind*, (Dell) 208.
6. Maria Montessori, *The Absorbent Mind*, (Dell) 167.
7. Maria Montessori, *Education and Peace*, (Dell) 38.

> Times have changed, and science has made great progress, and so has our work; but our principles have only been confirmed, and along with them our conviction that mankind can hope for a solution to its problems, among which the most urgent are those of peace and unity, only by turning its attention and energies to the discovery of the child and to the development of the great potentialities of the human personality in the course of its formation.[8]

The AMI/USA Journal: Spring 2018 featured an article titled "Moving Beyond Peace Education to Social Justice Education," by Daisy Han and Trisha Moquino. It specifically rejects Montessori's solution for peace:

> In the twentieth century, Dr. Maria Montessori used Cosmic Education as a way to educate humanity about the interconnectedness of all life. In the thick of wars and political aggression, Cosmic Education taught children to recognize the fundamental needs we all share and to respect the differences by which we meet those fundamental needs. However, because whole populations were displaced and the ways that whole groups of people have come to meet their needs were appropriated, access to peace is obstructed by systemic oppression. Cosmic, or peace education, while a beautiful theory, is incomplete without the historical context and connection to social justice. Cosmic and peace education requires that we develop in children and in ourselves an understanding of the history of racial and social injustice and the tools to dismantle inequity, in ways that are significantly different than the current practices in most Montessori schools and teacher training programs today.

My response: In other words, until those white kids are made to kneel, peace isn't possible.

> Together, as women of color in this field, we have felt the omission of this focus and we feel the impact of the omission of People of Color in the spaces and places where Montessori education is practiced, researched and taught. As Montessorians, we must ask ourselves the ways in which we practice peace education in our classrooms and what stories we share with our children. There is no doubt that Montessori education has the potential to serve as a liberating and decolonizing education; however, for this to be true, Montessorians must reflect on some uncomfortable truths: Who has historically received a Montessori education or Montessori teacher certification in America and why that has been the case?

---

8. Maria Montessori, "Foreword" of *The Discovery of the Child*.

> How have Montessorians perpetuated a false narrative of peace? At whose expense and why have only some children been able to receive this idea of peace education? Do we as Montessorians remind our children of those whose lands we inhabit? How can we feel peace in our hearts if we do not feel represented in the leadership of Montessori education? How do we, as a Montessori community, continue to amplify the voices of People of Color? Do we honor Dr. Montessori's charge of us as radical activists? [9]

My response: This was a racial diatribe. If she really cared about who was receiving Montessori certification, she would start a program to help more teachers receive Montessori training. Furthermore, Montessori did not say we should be radical political activists, "*Not in the service of any political or social creed should the teacher work...*" [10] and "*...a teacher should never forget that he is a teacher and that his mission is one of education.*" [11]

On November 15, 2020, there was a webinar on "Preparing Ourselves Spiritually and Mentally for Revolutionary Social Change." Here is the description:

> This webinar will address how to prepare spiritually and mentally to view all aspects of the Montessori experience through an Anti-racist, Anti-bias (ABAR) lens. ABAR work is not a curriculum, but a journey that begins with the preparation of the guiding adult.[12]

Sheri Bishop, Social Justice Advisor to AMI/USA and the webinar master, answered questions that were asked in the chat. One of the questions was "How do you see reparations happening?" Her answer:

> I think that reparations should be offered to the descendants of Africans that were enslaved in America. I think it would be up to a very diverse, well-educated group of scholars, anthropologists, historians, etc., to determine who would qualify to receive it.[13]

---

9. Daisy Han and Trisha Moquino, "Moving Beyond Peace Education," *AMI/USA Journal* (Spring 2018).
10. Maria Montessori, *To Educate the Human Potential*, 3.
11. Maria Montessori, *The Secret of Childhood*, (Montessori-Pierson) 153.
12. Sheri Bishop, "Preparing Ourselves Spiritually and Mentally," *AMI/USA*, November 20, 2015.
13. Ibid.

My response: What black students deserve today from Montessori educators is what all students have always deserved and many have received—a good, authentic Montessori education that treats them, and all their classmates, no matter who, with respect and as an individual with agency and intelligence. What they seem to want is revenge, and the destruction of the entire Montessori framework of respecting each child and individualism as their scalp. People in the United States who are alive now are not responsible for what happened over 160 years ago. Black people who are alive today are not responsible for the Black people who enslaved each other 160 years ago.[14] Plus, there are no Black people alive in the United States today who were/are enslaved. In fact, Black people and other minorities have been receiving reparations for decades at the expense of white Americans in the form of quotas and subsidies in the areas of college admissions, job acquisition and promotion, etc. When do these activists think white people will be done paying, and what does that have to do with educating each child as an individual with nurturing guidance and respect? It doesn't have anything to do with it.

If there are any holdover consequences from slavery, such as generational dysfunction and poverty, then the cure is surely a fair, nurturing, and respectful education that treats children as individuals for as many children as possible.

On July 30, 2021 AMI/USA had a Black Montessori Education Fund Anniversary Fundraiser.[15]

My response: What about other races? What about poor children? How about just a Montessori Education Fundraiser?

This is the AMI/USA Equity Statement written in 2020. It was prepared by Sheri L. Bishop. This statement was supported by AMI/USA Board members, members of the AMI/USA HRSJ Committee, AMI/USA operational staff members, and members from the larger Montessori community.[16]

---

14. The Historian, "Black Slave Owners – 10 Most Famous," *Have Fun With History*, December 22, 2022.

15. Chad Dennis, "Black Montessori Education Fund Anniversary Fundraiser," *Black Montessori Education Fund on Eventbrite*, July 30, 2021.

16. The AMI/USA Equity Statement 2020 was signed by Ayize Sabater, AMI/USA Executive Director; Mary Levy, Chair, AMI/USA Board of Directors; KaLinda Bass-Barlow, Chair, AMI/USA HRSJ Committee; Sheri L. Bishop, AMI/USA HRSJ Advisor; and Cierra Littlejohn, Elementary Guide and Montessori 9 Community Member.

Dr. Maria Montessori's call was to educate for peace. The charge for Association Montessori International of the United States (AMI/USA) is to promote global peace, guide the natural development of all children to allow them to realize their full human potential, and to recognize and uphold human rights for all through the application of Montessori principles. Montessori pedagogy was intended from its onset to be an aid to life and a tool for liberation and empowerment. Yet, we have been witnesses to, and participants in, behaviors that have silenced earnest protestations against bias and racism toward Black, Indigenous, and People of Color (BIPOC) and other marginalized groups. After nine of our members experienced a painful racial incident at the Montessori Refresher Course in Seattle, WA in early 2020, after living through the devastating televised death of George Floyd, and after watching the powerful social justice movement that changed global thought and demanded a shift in world-wide racial paradigms, we have been awakened.

Atonement

We live in a racialized society and we are socialized into a race-based culture. Racism is a socially transmitted disease passed down from generation to generation and is a social determinant of health that has a profound impact on the health status of children, adolescents, emerging adults, and their families. (Trent, Dooley, Dougé, 2019). Its legacy has yet to be reckoned with and the effects still live in our institutions, communities, homes, and even in the individuals that make up our collective organizations. We deeply regret that AMI/USA has allowed the social ill of racism to create barriers in our organizations and schools that do a disservice to the children we ultimately serve. We cannot continue to be complicit in this behavior. It stands in the way of transformational changes required to achieve true education for peace, justice, equity, diversity and inclusion throughout the organization and all Montessori communities.

Transformation

It is time that AMI/USA commits to deliberately and intentionally adopting values and practices that will transform our organization from one that has not been fully welcoming to all marginalized people, to one that embraces and shares power with all people. To realize meaningful and sustainable changes, we are taking action at the organizational level to create an anti-racist, anti-bias, equitable Montessori culture. We commit to providing the time and financial resources to have key stakeholders, including the Executive Director, members of the Board of Directors, the organizational staff, and the Human Rights and Social Justice Committee (HRSJ) advisors, receive on-going training that supports our awareness of our shared American history, interrogating personal biases and adverse racist behaviors, and developing effective skills to view all aspects of the organization through an anti-bias/anti-racist lens. We strive to honor and employ human rights and social justice values in all aspects of the organization and intentionally have those holding leadership and advisory roles include the historically suffocated voices of our colleagues. We will routinely examine organizational policies and practices that maintain patterns of structural racism that disadvantage BIPOC and others with overlapping intersectionalities. A proud affiliate of Association Montessori Internationale will consistently measure progress to inform professional development needs and organizational adaptations.

Advocacy and Hope

We value the lives, lived experiences, contributions, and talents of Black, Indigenous and People of Color (BIPOC) with whom we work and serve and are striving to establish an organizational ethos that prioritizes humanity. We understand that this evolution requires perpetual work. We acknowledge that building and maintaining an inclusive, racially equitable culture will be never-ending and that ever-lasting transformation requires courage, persistence, unwavering commitment, and individual and collective accountability. We encourage all members, especially those that identify as an ally, social justice activist, anti-bias/anti-racist educator, social justice healer and/or an artistic and creative storyteller, to lift your voices and together let us all participate in this transformational journey. "Today an urgent need imposes itself upon society: the reconstruction of methods in education and instruction, and he who fights for this cause, fights for human regeneration" (Montessori, 2014).[17]

My response: The purpose of Montessori schools is not to atone for the sins of people from long ago. Their purpose is to give children the education possible for self-fulfillment and happiness. No explanation is given about what happened at the refresher course. While Blacks, Indigenous and People of Color are valued, nothing is said about Whites or Asians. To be truly inclusive, all individuals should be valued.

---

17. AMI/USA, "AMI/USA Equity Statement," *AMI/USA*, February 11, 2021.

On November 2, 2020, there was an Anti-Bias & Anti-Racist (ABAR) Administrator workshop to equip administrators "with actionable steps to either start or strengthen your ABAR school culture. Administrators will learn about being an ABAR gatekeeper, how to strengthen family partnerships, and create a space for staff to hold one another accountable."[18]

On February 24, 2021, Sheri Bishop presented a talk called "Racial Equity: An Important Call to Action for Administrators and Board of Directors."[19]

On March 20, 2023, Sara Bloomberg, LGBTQIA+ and social advocacy Montessori trainer, consultant, and teacher educator, moderated an open discussion with Olli Lehman, M.A. and Ashley McLean, both Montessori colleagues, on Zoom to discuss Exploring Gender Expansiveness in the Montessori Environment. She started a group called The Queer Montessorians[20] and a Facebook group called Queer Montessorians.[21] She said, "For as long as I can remember I have always wanted to advocate for queer children, and really anyone who questions their gender identity or sexuality."[22] Here is her description from her website:

> Sara Bloomberg (a.k.a. Seaweed Rubinstein) M. Ed, is the head of Protea Montessori Consultants, a consulting company that strives to bring gender diversity, gender equity and the LGBTQA+ curriculum to educators across the globe. Sara was the founder of the Early Childhood Division at the St Augustine Public Montessori School and is AMS Credentialed (Early Childhood). Sara was the founding Director at Battery Park Montessori in New York and served on the faculty of West Side Montessori's Teacher Education Program as a Field Consultant and Math Instructor. Sara has consulted for schools in New York and St Augustine. Sara is incredibly passionate about collaborating with educators and parents to help them support and guide LGBTQA children and teachers in the Early Childhood and Lower Elementary years. Sara uses "they, them and their" pronouns.[23]

---

18. Amelia Sherwood, "The Anti-Bias & Anti-Racist Administrator Workshop," *AMI/USA*, November 2, 2020.

19. Sheri Bishop, "Racial Equity: An Important Call to Action," *AMI/USA*, February 24, 2021.

20. Sara Bloomberg interviewed by *The Male Montessorian*, May 31, 2019.

21. Queer Montessori, "Facebook Group: queer montessorians," *Facebook*.

22. Sara Bloomberg interviewed by *West Side Montessori*.

23. Sara Bloomberg interviewed by *The Male Montessorian*, May 31, 2019.

From Bloomberg's website:

> Sara: In 2017 I taught children ages 6–9. One day my wife came to visit me at lunchtime. This caused some excitement and also some consternation specifically with one child who exclaimed: "*But you can't have two queens, you always need a king and a queen!*" She was visibly upset at the notion that two women were living together in the same house without a man. At first, I didn't respond. I didn't have to because her friends jumped in and said: "*That's not true, you can have two queens or two kings living together in the same house.*" Many others piped in offering more ideas to her. "*Two women can get married, so can two men and they can have children.*" "*Even a prince and a prince can live together too!*" Another child chimed in "*President Barack Obama says it's ok too. And it is ok.*" After a while, I took the experience one step further by asking, "*Does a king have to be a man? Does a queen have to be a woman?*" From there, we had lively discussions about gender identity and labels. The child who initially was perturbed seemed much more at ease with the notion of two women living together. Her reaction was the perfect springboard for us to incorporate books about gender identity and diversity into the curriculum.[24]

My response: "Does a king have to be a man? Does a queen have to be a woman?" This is a perfect example of confusing a child about reality. Chapter 1 explained the importance of forming concepts accurately. If words have no meaning in reality, thinking is thwarted. Anyone who tries to confuse a child about gender does not want to be judged on his choices, so would like to indoctrinate children in order to be accepted. This is the mentality of tyrants who want a society of people so empty-headed they can't judge and will follow the whims of a despot.

March 31, 2023, AMI/USA sponsored Transgender Visibility Day. "As a prelude to this day of recognition, our goal at AMI/USA is to explore gender expansiveness in Montessori settings… Please join us as Sara Bloomberg moderates an open discussion with Olli Lehman, M.A. and Ashley McLean, both Montessori colleagues who are personally and professionally close to this important topic."[25]

My response: Totally inappropriate to "explore gender expansiveness in Montessori settings."

On January 29, 2024, Sheri Bishop moderated a discussion in a

---

24. Sara Bloomberg interviewed by *The Male Montessorian*, May 31, 2019..
25. Sara Bloomberg, "Exploring Gender Expansiveness," *AMI/USA*, March 20, 2023.

webinar called "Are Montessori Educators Barely Awake, Woke, or Too Woke for Our Time and Place?"

On April 28, 2024, AMI/USA had a webinar series on social justice. The topics listed on their website were:

- "Remembering Indigenous Voices in the Classroom"
- "The Anti-Bias and Anti-Racist Administrator"
- "Preparing Ourselves for Revolutionary Change"
- "De-Centering Whiteness in Montessori Spaces." [26]

Compounding its corruption, AMI/USA has participated in changing history. [27] On November 24, 2022 they published an article entitled "Gratitude for the National Day of Mourning," [28] that was posted on Facebook [29] with an explanation: "This event serves to educate all Americans about the false narrative of the Thanksgiving story." The article does not specify the false narrative, but it does include this paragraph:

> History wants us to believe that the Indian was a savage, illiterate, uncivilized animal. A history that was written by an organized, disciplined people, to expose us as an unorganized and undisciplined entity. Two distinctly different cultures met. One thought they must control life; the other believed life was to be enjoyed, because nature decreed it. Let us remember, the Indian is and was just as human as the white man. The Indian feels pain, gets hurt, and becomes defensive, has dreams, bears tragedy and failure, suffers from loneliness, needs to cry as well as laugh. He, too, is often misunderstood.

My response: Is the false narrative that Indians were made out to be savages when they were not? The fact is that there *were* tribes [30] (not all) that were savage, violent, and uncivilized during that time period (brutal slaughters, rapes, tortures, scalping people alive) just as there *were* some Europeans [31] that committed some horrific acts (also scalping people

---

26. AMI/USA, "Social Justice Webinar Series," *AMI/USA*, September 8, 2020.

27. Charlotte Cushman, "Montessori Organization Debunks Thanksgiving," *American Thinker*, November 27, 2022.

28. Siobhan Growing Elm Brown, "Gratitude for The National Day of Mourning," *AMI/USA*, November 24, 2022.

29. AMI/USA, "National Day of Mourning," *Facebook: AMI/USA*, November 24, 2022.

30. Jonathan Foreman, "The truth Johnny Depp wants to hide," *The Daily Mail*, August 18, 2013.

31. Mark Oliver, "Horrific Facts About Scalping On The American Frontier," *Listverse*,

alive). And the U.S. government [32] didn't always treat the Indians fairly (breaking treaties), but history has a context, and during that time, mankind was in the process of becoming more civilized. You can't condemn historical people because they didn't know what we know in the 21st century—the concept of individual rights and respecting those rights instead of resorting to violence or some type of destruction.

The Thanksgiving story is not about portraying Indians in a negative light. Thanksgiving is a celebration of peace and friendship that was real, it actually took place, between settlers and Indians. The Pilgrims and the Indians chose to celebrate their accomplishment of abundance of food together. They got along, there was some peace between them. It was good, it was something to celebrate. It is important to note that the Pilgrims invited Indians to the first Thanksgiving, and there were more Indians present than Pilgrims. It would seem that they had a friendly relationship.

To vilify Thanksgiving by celebrating the "Day of Mourning" shows a lack of respect for the generosity and productiveness celebrated during that first momentous occasion between the early settlers and the Indians. Thanksgiving is a time that all Americans (which includes Indians) can celebrate a heritage of which they all can be very proud. At the first Thanksgiving, everyone came together in peace. Why would anyone try to ruin a tradition that was based on a festivity that included both cultures from the outset? Today we do have an understanding of individual rights, and the attempt to raise one group by vilifying another deserves denunciation. It isn't the Thanksgiving story that is pushing a false narrative.

On the comment thread under the article, I posted an article called The Tale of the Pilgrims—Why It Needs to Be Taught, that explains why children need to learn the history of their own country.[33] I was told by a Montessorian, "… you seem to misunderstand the whole root of the Montessori philosophy. Montessori is about anti-racism, not the perspective you share…"

AMI is the organization whose purpose originally was to keep the

---

July 16, 2017.

Jonathan Foreman, "The truth Johnny Depp wants to hide," *The Daily Mail*, August 18, 2013.

32. Wikipedia, "Trail of Tears," *Wikipedia*, October 16, 2024.

33. Charlotte Cushman, "The Tale of the Pilgrims," *American Thinker*, November 25, 2010.

Montessori Method pure. Is AMI/USA really teaching their teachers that Montessori is about anti-racism? Montessori thought that education should direct itself toward developing the individual child, and that the Montessori Method is about the cognitive development of the child's mind so that he learns how to reason. That isn't being taught anymore? Aren't teachers reading Montessori's books? Her entire books?

On that thread, an owner of a Montessori school said that she does not teach the Thanksgiving story. Eliminating an important side of history is a form of indoctrination. What happened happened. Just because there were tribes that were savage and Europeans that were brutal, doesn't take away the fact that some were not, or say anything about people becoming more civilized since. Our ancestors lived 400 years ago, and we are not responsible for what they did, nor do the sins of some negate the virtue of others, nor do their actions or attitudes in the past determine ours now. To say otherwise is to deny that humans have free will, which Montessori clearly supported.[34] The denial of free will is determinism, the idea that our actions and values are determined by something other than our own choices, and that's the foundation for racism.

We can be grateful, however, for the civilization that was created that we all benefit from now. Yes, we all benefit, everyone. No matter what our heritage, whether of European or early American Indian descent, we all benefit from freedom. I would be surprised to hear that anyone wants to go back to a time without airplanes, cars, light bulbs, television, antibiotics, warm homes in the winter, technological advancements, and so on.

American Montessori Society (AMS)

The American Montessori Society is another major Montessori organization which runs training centers for teachers and certifies schools. AMS was founded in 1960 in the United States by Nancy Rambusch. Americans had been introduced to Montessori education in the early 1900s but their initial excitement and support for it waned due to John Dewey's negativity towards the method. Progressive education dominated most schools, but discontent with it began to grow by the 1950s. Nancy Rambusch sought an alternative and attended the Tenth International Montessori Congress. While there, she met Mario Montessori, Maria Montessori's son, who urged Rambusch to take the Montessori

---

34. Maria Montessori, *The Absorbent Mind*, (Dell) 271.

coursework and bring Montessori education to the United States. That is exactly what she did.³⁵

Six and a half decades later, Rambusch's work has been turned on its head. In the Fall of 2016, AMS published, 'Social Justice Education in an Urban Charter Montessori School' in Vol. 2, No. 2 of its Journal of Montessori Research. The abstract states:

> As the Montessori Method continues its expansion in public education, a social justice lens is needed to analyze its contributions and limitations, given the increase in racial and socioeconomic diversity in the United States. Furthermore, much of the work in Social Justice Education (SJE) focuses on classroom techniques and curriculum, overlooking the essential work of school administrators and parents, whose work significantly influences the school community. The current study applied an SJE framework to the efforts of one urban, socioeconomically and racially integrated Montessori charter school. We examined the extent to which SJE principles were incorporated across the school community, using an inductive, qualitative, case-study approach that included meetings, surveys, focus groups, and interviews. Administrators quickly adopted a system-wide approach, but parents—often color-blind or minimizing of the relevance of race—consistently resisted. Study results imply a continued need for an institutional approach, not solely a classroom or curricular focus, when integrating social justice into Montessori schools.³⁶

My response: Overlooking "the essential work of school administrators and parents," isn't authentic Montessori education. The last sentence sounds like the classroom is supposed to take a backseat to an institutional approach of shaping outcomes. Of course, the parents minimized the relevance of race because a person's character isn't determined by race. As Montessori said, the child develops his own character. Departing from a focus on the child as an individual is in direct conflict with Montessori's method. Wishing parents were more race obsessed and less color blind is an extraordinary thing to say.

The AMS website has a page website called "Gender Diversity and Inclusivity in the Classroom" dated the summer of 2017. It begins by defining the terms transgender, gender nonconforming, cisgender, gender

---

35. American Montessori Society, "History of the American Montessori Society," *AMS*.
36. Kira Banks and R. Alex Maixner, "Social Justice Education," *Journal of Montessori Research* 2, no. 2 (2016).

affirmative, gender constancy, gender inclusivity, gender variance, and gender diversity. Their position on all these "genders" is that they all should be validated:

> On its website (amshq.org), the American Montessori Society lists six values that guide its work. In this essay, we touch upon at least three of those values (inclusiveness, diversity, and respect) as we offer suggestions on incorporating gender diversity into an already existing framework of inclusivity, in order to create a safe and affirming space for children. We understand gender diversity as the notion that issues of diversity should include gender in all its variations, and gender inclusivity as the idea that all gender identities and expressions should be validated and included.[37]

Then they cover topics such as pronouns and bathroom usage among other things. One of the main messages is to affirm and always encourage the child's "authentic" self, which means the child can identify however he wants, use whatever bathroom he wants, use whatever pronouns he wants, and so on.

In 2020, Sara Bloomberg was elected to the AMS board of directors.[38] (For more information about her see the previous section.)

In 2020, the AMS website announced that AMI/USA and AMS released a joint social justice publication:

> As leaders of the world's two most impactful Montessori organizations—the American Montessori Society and the Association Montessori International/USA (which represents the Association Montessori Internationale in the United States)—we are thrilled to share with you a publication we co-created for you, our members. Collaborating on this resource was a unique opportunity for us to come together in honor of Dr. Maria Montessori as we approach her 150th birthday anniversary on August 31, 2020.
>
> The publication, *Montessori Collaborative World Review: The Montessori Roots of Social Justice,* provides a multi-perspective exploration of the Montessori roots of social justice—from adolescent education as a key to social change, to the challenges and dreams of Montessori in South Africa, to selecting anti-bias children's books, and everything in

---

37. Charles Goehring, "Gender Diversity and Inclusivity in the Classroom," *AMS*, Summer 2017.

38. American Montessori Society, "Election Results: AMS Board of Directors," *AMS*, June 4, 2020.

between. The manifold voices—there are nearly 40 authors representing a variety of affiliations—bring not only depth of thought, but also breadth.

My response: Social change is a result of intellectual stability and strength. Thus, Montessori focuses on building the inner confidence and strength of the child.

On August 12, 2021, AMS put on a webinar called "Critical Race Theory: Talking Through the Confusion." The panelists were Dr. Valaida (Val) L. Wise, adjunct professor at Johns Hopkins University, and Wendy Shenk-Evans, executive director of MPPI. (MPPI is the policy arm of AMI/USA and AMS, and serves as the voice for Montessori policy.) They "provided insight from an academic and policy perspective on Critical Race Theory and the implications of the current dialogue for the Montessori community." [39]

From the webinar: Critical race theory (CRT) is defined as looking at understanding power structures and imbalances, how they are reproduced over time, and how people can positively impact social systems to promote change. CRT started at the Frankfurt school in Germany in the 1920s, and it isn't true that CRT is built on Marxism. Black Lives Matter (BLM) is teaming up with CRT.

My response: It is true that CRT is built on Marxism. As we learned earlier, the Frankfurt school taught Marxism; it was a Marxist school. CRT is Marxism repackaged for the West, where class was not an animating issue, so class struggle was replaced with race, sex, culture, and skin color. BLM has partnered with the Marxist CRT spawned movement, which was clear on their website for anyone who cared to look when BLM was founded. Furthermore, the BLM movement founders themselves were openly Marxists.

Ayo Tometi, one of BLM's founders, has worked to advance social justice,[40] and has participated in social movements, ultimately under the influence of Stuart Hall, a Marxist sociologist,[41] and other Marxists.[42] According to her biography, she is "a student of liberation theology [Marxism merged with Catholicism] and her practice is in the tradition

---

39. Valaida (Val) L. Wise, "Critical Race Theory," *American Montessori Society*, August 19, 2021.
40. Ayo Tometi, "Biography," *Ayo Tometi*, 2024.
41. Wikipedia, "Stuart Hall (cultural theorist)," *Wikipedia*, 2024.
42. WebArchive.org, "Our Co-founders," *Black Lives Matter*.

of Ella Baker, informed by Stuart Hall, [a woman named] bell hooks, and Black Feminist thinkers."[43]

Patrice Cullors was another BLM co-founder. She was heavily influenced after high school when she attended a "social justice camp" and studied Mao, Marx, and Lenin. She said that Eric Mann took her "under his wing." Mann was arrested for many violent crimes, including shooting at a police building, and was charged with attempted murder. It has been reported that he detests America, trains revolutionaries, and praises the university as the place for radicalization. In 2021, Patrisse Cullors was an executive director of the Black Lives Matter Global Network Foundation. Initially, it's financial support "flowed through a nonprofit co-chaired by Susan Rosenberg, a co-founder of the May 19th Communist Organization, a domestic terrorist group active in the 1980's." Rosenberg didn't think that using political violence made her a terrorist, and Cullors expressed similar sentiments.[44] In 2021, Cullors revealed the truth about BLM, saying, "We are trained Marxists."[45]

The third co-founder, Alicia Garza, has been on the board at the School of Unity and Liberation (SOUL), a radical-left activist training organization based in California. Her description at Influence Watch states "Alicia Garza, a self-described Marxist and co-founder of the Black Lives Matter movement, interned at SOUL in 2003, where she studied Marxism and learned grassroots organizing techniques."[46] She went beyond just studying Marxism into supporting authentic Marxism-Leninism:

> When I trained in sociology, we would read Marx, and we would read de Tocqueville, and we would read all these economic theorists, but in a void. It never got mentioned in those classes that social movements all over the world have used Marx and Lenin as a foundation to interrupt these systems that are really negatively impacting the majority of people.[47]

She speaks favorably about communist revolution and revolution being

---

43. Scott Walter, "The Founders of Black Lives Matter," *Capital Research*, April 5, 2021.
44. Ibid.
45. Patrisse Cullors interviewed with Martyn Iles, "We Are Trained Marxists," June 19, 2020, *YouTube*.
46. Influence Watch, "School of Unity and Liberation (SOUL)," *Influence Watch*, 2024.
47. Scott Walter, "The Founders of Black Lives Matter," *Capital Research*, April 5, 2021.

her goal. Garza wrote an introduction to the book, *Revolution in the Air: Sixties Radicals Turn to Lenin, Mao and Che.*[48]

So much for trying to pretend that BLM isn't Marxist, and not just that, but a means of revolution. This fact has been covered up with the excuse that not all people who have joined their movement are Marxists. It doesn't matter. In any movement, it is the leaders who drive it. The goals and activities are clearly revolutionary, such as protesting violently, defunding police, making city leaders kneel, and threatenings of more violence. If some people didn't understand what they were joining, well, that is just more evidence of the need to teach children to think.

From the webinar: We must be responsive to all cultures so the child feels significant. We must honor where he came from. A student's culture must be sustained in the classroom, otherwise you aren't recognizing him. Playing rap music or speaking another language in the classroom are examples of sustaining cultures. The work of students must be culturally relevant for them. It is "…incumbent upon teachers, especially white teachers, to help students be culturally verbose so that they can walk both worlds and understand their own as well as the worlds of others."

My response: What about the American culture? Don't American children count? It sounds like the message is don't let them be Americans. What if the teacher were trying to sustain the cultures of six or more children at the same time? Are they all supposed to speak different languages in the classroom? Separating the children by dividing them into groups, will balkanize the classroom. The Montessori materials are universal; they are for all children.

Different cultures are acknowledged in the Montessori classroom where one area of the classroom is devoted to learning about countries and cultures from all over the world. This is done with the globes, maps, culture boxes, music, and books. However, a foreign student's culture should not be "sustained" at school. When a foreigner goes to another country, it is not up to the citizens of that country to change to accommodate him. It is up to him to assimilate, else what happens to that culture? What happens to the children born in America if every culture but theirs is sustained?

The patently false assumption is that a child cannot "feel significant" unless he belongs to a group (his culture, race, sex, etc.). This makes the group more important than the individual. If the goal is to help a child

---

48. Scott Walter, "The Founders of Black Lives Matter," *Capital Research*, April 5, 2021.

to feel secure, to help him learn so he feels confident in his own mind, the focus needs to be on the child, not his culture of origin.

> *He who interprets the children in their occupations in order to make them learn some predetermined thing; he who makes them cease the study of arithmetic to pass on to that of geography and the like, thinking it is important to direct their culture, confuses the means with the end and destroys the man for a vanity.* <u>*All that which is necessary to direct is not the culture of man, but the man himself.*</u> [49] (Emphasis added.)

From the webinar: The children are not taught CRT in school. The teacher implements the ideas of the theory, but does not teach the ideas.

My response: The theory may not be taught, but it is happening in practice. In other words, the claim is that because social justice ideology isn't taught *as an ideology,* it is not present in schools. This is a cover up. On Substack, Holly Mathnerd, a commenter, explains that:

> Montessori schools don't *teach* her philosophies. Students don't typically learn the history of her ideas or the reasoning behind why their classrooms are set up the way they are. Many students have no idea that "Montessori" is a person's name, much less that it's the name of a person whose philosophies and ideas are the reason behind every aspect of their school experience. That's because Montessori schools *practice* her ideas. They are living, breathing entities in which her ideas are embodied and practiced. The consequences of her ideas are integrated into the minds and hearts of her students, becoming part of their personalities and shaping their deepest selves as they grow.[50]

From the webinar: CRT is not racist. CRT looks at systems and how systems perpetuate racism in the United States. Some states are passing laws restricting teaching CRT, i.e., the 1619 project. The Declaration of Independence and Constitution are racist documents. The bills being passed in states banning CRT are racist.

My response: If CRT isn't being taught, then why be upset that states are passing laws restricting it? By what inverted logic is banning race separatism and race obsession considered racist?

---

49. Maria Montessori, *Spontaneous Activity in Education,* (Robert Bentley) 180.
50. Holly Mathnerd, "The Queering of the American Child," *Holly's Substack* (blog), February 16, 2024.

The 1619 project claims that the Revolutionary War was fought to preserve slavery in North America, that all of America's success was because of slave labor, and that the country began when the first slaves stepped onto the shore and not when the Founders declared independence. It is made-up and has been completely discredited. There is nothing in the founding documents or letters from that time period reporting it. There is nothing racist about the Declaration of Independence: the founding document guarantees the rights of all individuals. It eventually led to the abolition of slavery, both the 13th amendment to the U.S. Constitution which ended involuntary servitude, and the 14th amendment which ensured the full rights and citizenship of the freed slaves.

From the webinar: The reason why there is resistance to CRT is that people are afraid of losing power.

My response: No, they disagree with it. As you saw above, the parent resistance is because they think it's racist. In addition, people in this country have the right to speak and have their voices heard, and that isn't acknowledged by CRT advocates. Instead, people who disagree with CRT are smeared as racist or bigoted. But if you were to ask me if I want freedom loving people to lose power to racist Marxists, then no, I don't. Guilty as charged!

From the webinar: Someone in the chat asked this question: If there is nothing scary about CRT, why should we be so quick to assure families we aren't teaching it? Isn't it true that when you define CRT, many of the basic ideas are things that we actually do want our children to learn? The answer given:

> Systemic and historical racism is real and creates power imbalances and inequities today. So please don't misunderstand that we shouldn't teach our children the truth. But the reality is you're not teaching critical race theory. It is a very high-level academic initiative where you are critiquing and talking and it's writing about each thing so that's not what we're teaching children, but are we teaching children the truth about racism in the United States? Absolutely. And critical race theory helps us to understand that as adults and as academics. But what you will really be doing is doing culturally responsive and culturally sustaining pedagogy where you are introducing the idea and asking the question the system that would be appropriate.

My response: This is the claim that CRT isn't being taught, but that children are only learning the "truth" about history—which is that there is systemic racism. Instead of presenting the facts about history and letting the children form their own conclusions, the children are being indoctrinated. If CRT informs the teachers so they can then teach about racism in America according to CRT, then CRT is being taught whether you mention "CRT" or not.

From the webinar: "Race in America is so very complicated because you have to first agree that it happens, and then be willing to hear the research that tells you why it's happening. And then have the empathy and the wherewithal to sacrifice what is needed to do something about it."

My response: This is incorrect epistemology. The conclusion was made first before looking at reality. This is not at all Montessori pedagogy. This can't be emphasized enough—reality is the starting point of all knowledge. To repeat what Montessori said,

> *... in order to develop the imagination, it is necessary for everyone first of all to put himself in contact with reality.* [51]

First, you identify the facts of reality; you don't start by just agreeing with somebody. That pushes the notion that reality is whatever somebody else says it is. No reasonable person would say there isn't still some residue of racism, but it is not the major problem of our country. Yet this is the focus of CRT, and it is highly discriminatory of White and Asian races. And CRT partisans claim they are not racist.

On January 18, 2022, AMS posted the Top Five Powerful ABAR (Anti-Bias, Anti-Racist) Podcasts. Here are the first three paragraphs on the page:

> ABAR stands for Anti-bias, Antiracist. It is a method for learning about our own bias, prejudice, privilege, and oppression with the end goal of creating a racially equitable society. When students learn about inclusivity at school, the goal is that they take their learnings into the community to counteract systemic oppression and appropriation. Of course, it's important to continue these conversations at home, but school is key because, historically speaking, we learn a sugar-coated, Eurocentric history.
>
> Quite frankly, most public school history courses celebrate murderers

---

51. Maria Montessori, *Spontaneous Activity in Education*, (Robert Bentley) 250.

as victors and forget the rest. When we purposefully exclude the horrors that white people have perpetuated onto BIPOC communities for hundreds of years, we knowingly build a system that upholds systemic racism and oppression. These systems only continue to perpetuate racial inequity, cultural appropriation, and microaggressions. (In other words, if history is power, and history has been white-washed, *uh-oh*, we then unfortunately equate whiteness with power.) With awareness, continued education, and sustained action, I deeply hope we create the equity we wish to see.

If you're white, like me, I'm really grateful that you're here. I believe it's quite literally our moral and societal obligation to dive into ABAR work. We need to unlearn our deeply rooted biases, we need to have important conversations with our white peers about race, and we need to actively take steps to dismantle and reconstruct the systemically racist society that directly benefits us. We need to be socially aware as to not further appropriate other cultures or continue to spread microaggressions that were likely commonplace in our houses growing up. As educators, it is also crucial that we don't allow microaggressions and appropriation into classroom culture. Keep in mind, there is no shame in learning and changing your opinions, actions, and words as you evolve in your ABAR learnings.[52]

My response: These statements are biased, and assume everyone is biased and racist. The writer is promoting racism against Whites with the claims that white people have visited horrors (murders) on people of color for hundreds of years. All the white people that fought and died in the Civil War to end slavery, all the white people who ended slavery in the United States, the British who ended the slave trade globally, the slave trade in Africa by Africans, the Arab slave trade that enslaved whites and blacks, all the white people who voted to make people of color citizens, and white people who treat people of color with respect—all those facts are carefully ignored. Most importantly, all the white people, those Europeans, who signed the Declaration of Independence and fought in the Revolutionary War for the founding idea that allows opinions to be expressed are ignored. There are people of all races who are racist, but only Whites are mentioned. Notice the desire to "actively take steps to dismantle and reconstruct the systemically racist society." In other words, let's dismantle the United States. (Again, a Marxist goal.)

---

52. Kat St. Pierre, "Top 5 Powerful ABAR Podcasts," *AMS* (blog), January 18, 2022.

On June 5, 2023, AMS published an article called "Pride Month Reads: LGBTQIA+ Stories for Children and Teens," which includes a recommended reading list for preschool children, elementary aged children, and teens. A few of the titles are: *My Moms Love Me, The Rainbow Parade, Kind Like Marsha: Learning from LGBTQ+ Leaders, ABC Pride, If You're a Kid Like Gavin: The True Story of a Young Trans Activist, 6 Times We Almost Kissed (And One Time We Did)*, and *Queer Ducks (and Other Animals): The Natural World of Animal Sexuality*.[53]

My response: These topics are only appropriate for adults. The books present only one view of sexually controversial subjects to children who do not have the context or development to be thinking about any of this, which is indoctrination.

On July 26, 2023, AMS posted on its website an article titled Banned Books: "The Most Frequently Challenged Books and Why." It includes these two paragraphs at the end:

> At issue is the fact that children's emotional and academic levels vary so much that censoring a book for mature content might not be right for all children in one class or grade. In addition, not every family shares the same political or religious beliefs. Whether or not a book is offensive depends very much on political and religious ideologies. When communities are diverse, made up of people with varying beliefs, then disagreements about what is "proper" or "moral" for children will often become a source of contention. However, in a social-media infused world, parents need to ask themselves how insular they desire and believe they can or want to keep their child.
>
> Banning books with difficult subject matter does not open the opportunity for discussion and encourage students to develop critical thinking. Challenged or banned books often offer a chance for parents to "promote open access to ideas, both of which are keys to raising a lifelong reader." A parent's involvement in teaching their child how to navigate the world is crucial. Parents are not only role models; they are interpreters for their children in a complex world where events are shaping the very societies their children will face as adults. Teaching children how to understand different viewpoints increases their critical thinking and empathy—skills they will most likely need more than ever in the future.[54]

---

53. V. Kulikow, "Pride Month Reads: LGBTQIA+," *AMS*, June 05, 2023.

54. V. Kulikow, "The Most Frequently Challenged Books and Why," *AMS* (blog), July 26, 2023.

My response: Is this saying there is no objectivity involved in deciding if a child is ready for certain topics? After all, we Montessorians do not present children with work for which they are not ready. The point is that the child needs to be intellectually and emotionally mature enough to be able to understand the book, understand context, and judge the morals (or lack thereof) in the book. Furthermore, pornography is never appropriate in school. It has no purpose other than to present sex as ugly and trite.

A keynote speaker at the AMS conference in 2024 was Dr. Ibram X Kendi, described as an anti-racism expert, who spoke about anti-racism. Among many other things, he was the founding director at the Boston University Center for Antiracist Research, an advocate for an antiracist constitutional amendment, and author of several books for children and adults on anti-racism. One for adults was a best seller, *How to Be An Antiracist*, another was a children's book called *Goodnight Racism*.[55]

My response: I ask where are the keynote speakers who talk about individualism or Montessori's concept of a confident, normal child? Focusing on racism fosters the notion that everyone is racist. It focuses all children on skin color as a basis for judging each other and themselves.

The mission statement for AMS states that social justice is one of its areas of involvement. AMS has an Anti-Bias, Antiracist Statement:

> The American Montessori Society is committed to interrogating ourselves and investigating our past practices, recognizing, addressing, and eradicating all current forms of racism and systemic oppression within our organization, and supporting our members in doing the same in their schools, programs, and practices. We recognize that an understanding of racism and bias varies across individuals, and engaging in transformational change requires courage, trust, empathy, and understanding.[56]

One of its strategic priorities is inclusion/equity.

AMS has Anti-Bias, Antiracist Affinity Groups.[57] An Anti-Bias, Antiracist Affinity Group focuses on promoting anti-racism and anti-biasism in Montessori schools and classrooms. "Affinity groups may

---

55. Dan Kalleres, "A Montessori Educator Reflects," *AMS* (blog), February 01, 2023.
56. American Montessori Society, "The Mission of the American Montessori Society" *AMS*.
57. American Montessori Society, "AMS Affinity Groups,"*AMS*.

form to drive change, provide a space for safe and open dialogue, and offer opportunities to solve particular issues." The groups also sponsor workshops, webinars, and online courses. One of these Affinity Groups is called The Montessorians of Color Affinity Group: A Safe Space for BIPOC.[58] "This group centers and amplifies the work and lives of Montessorians of Color." There is also the Español Affinity Group for Spanish speaking people and the Intersectionality/Inclusivity Discussion Group which focuses on marginalized identities.

My response: By promoting "anti-racist and anti-bias in Montessori schools and classrooms," the assumption is that racism and bias is pervasive, systemic and due to Eurocentricity. The focus should be on the development of each individual child instead.

AMS has an Anti-bias, Antiracist (ABAR) Certificate Program, too. The description reads:

> The AMS Anti-Bias, Antiracist (ABAR) Certificate Program provides a thorough examination of ABAR education to support Montessori schools and classrooms in creating just and equitable spaces for all. This program responds to Maria Montessori's mandate that we engage in a *systematic study of self.*

Some of the topics include: Unpacking Our Identities; Gender Fluidity, Neurodiversity, and Ableism; Power, Privilege, and Oppression in Montessori Environments; Curriculum Violence; and Working for Equity in Montessori Institutions. Among the outcomes are to "discover the deeply-rooted connections between ABAR education and Montessori philosophy" and to "deepen your knowledge of culturally responsive instruction and its impact on academic learning and the social emotional health of your students."[59]

My response: The social emotional health of students is reliant upon their intellectual health.

On August 15 and 22, 2024, AMS sponsored an Equity Examined Half-Day Virtual Workshop. Here is the description:

> Join us for a half-day virtual workshop to deepen your anti-bias antiracist

---

58. Heather White, "The Montessorians of Color Affinity Group," *AMS*, February 06, 2023.

59. American Montessori Society, "Anti-bias, Antiracist (ABAR) Certificate Program," *AMS*.

teaching practice and leadership. You will learn thoughtful strategies for using the Equity Examined tool and leave with ideas and action steps designed to move your school toward its ABAR mission. This session will provide an in-depth opportunity to explore Equity Examined with members of the Montessori community to help you and your organization create a more inclusive and equitable Montessori environment for everyone. [60]

My response: Assuming that teachers need to become more anti-biased and anti-racist and that schools do not encompass everyone is itself a bias.

An AMS accredited school for ages 18 months to 12 years in Boulder, Colorado has a page on its website called Diversity Resources. It lists anti-racist, anti-bias books for children, and also lists resources such as articles, videos, and webinars for adults. Their four goals for anti-bias education are identity, diversity, justice, and activism. [61]

My response: I saw nothing on that website about individuality.

A Montessori school in Baltimore, Maryland for children ages 18 months through 8th grade, accredited by AMS, has four goals of anti-bias education on their website. The first goal is identity:

> Adding to early childhood education's long-term commitment to nurturing each child's individual and personal identity, <u>anti-bias education emphasizes the important idea of nurturing children's social or group identities</u>. Children will learn accurate, respectful language to describe who they and others are. <u>Social identities include but are not limited to gender, racial, ethnic, cultural, religious, and economic class groups.</u> A strong sense of both individual and group identities is the foundation for the three other core anti-bias goals. (Emphasis added.) [62]

My response: The development of a child's personal identity comes first and foremost. Most of this sounds like Marxism, including dividing children into groups that they didn't choose. The school has no business highlighting all those differences other than the fact that boys are boys and girls are girls.

---

60. American Montessori Society, "Equity Examined Workshop," *AMS*, August 15 and 22, 2024.

61. Jarrow Montessori School, "Diversity Resources," *Jarrow Montessori School.*

62. Greenspring Montessori School, "Diversity, Equity, Inclusion, and Belonging," *Green Spring Montessori.*

National Center for Montessori in the Public Sector (NCMPS)

From their website:

> There are more than 500 public Montessori schools in the U.S., including district, magnet, and charter programs, and that number is growing fast as the education world recognizes and seeks out the proven effectiveness and depth of the Montessori approach. The National Center for Montessori in the Public Sector (NCMPS) maintains a database of public Montessori programs in all 50 states (and Washington, D.C.), and new listings are added monthly. Public Montessori schools are typically larger than private programs, so these 500+ schools can serve an estimated 125,000 children from ages three to eighteen.[63]

NCMPS is committed to equity:

> The National Center for Montessori in the Public Sector recognizes structural racism, inequality, and violence inherent in American social and political life, and stands in solidarity with all those who are working for change.[64]

Their website is full of recommended equity resources. Topics include but are not limited to critical race theory, anti-bias education, oppression, racism, and social change. There are LGBTQIA+ resources and sources for White people. The anti-bias section for White people includes many books, articles, podcasts, and videos. A few of the titles are: "White Privilege: Unpacking the Invisible Knapsack," "Who Gets to Be Afraid in America?," "America's Racial Contract Is Killing Us," "Raising White Kids," and "How White Parents Can Talk To Their Kids About Race."[65]

Montessori for Social Justice (MSJ)

Founded in 2013, Montessori for Social Justice is committed to "social justice, racial equity, and an anti-bias, antiracist application of Montessori pedagogy." Their mission statement:

---

63. National Center for Montessori in the Public Sector, "A Home for Public Montessori," *National Center for Montessori in the Public Sector*, 2024.

64. National Center for Montessori in the Public Sector, "Equity," *National Center for Montessori in the Public Sector*, 2024.

65. Ibid.

We support the creation of sustainable learning environments that dismantle systems of oppression, amplify the voices of the Global Majority, and cultivate partnerships to liberate the human potential.[66]

My response: The obvious objective is to create Soviet style youth activists primed and launched to agitate for their cause.

In June 22–25, 2023, MSJ had a conference entitled "Imagining Liberation…Honoring Our Humanity." The opening keynote speaker, Dr. Nicole Evans, criticized states that were banning books, ending DEI initiatives, banning trans children from sports, and banning gender affirming care. The general message from this conference was that we all have biases and systemic racism is a problem.[67]

My response: Certain books are restricted for children in schools because they are inappropriate. Is it possible to not be racist? If it is not possible, then what's the point of anti-racism? If it is possible, then they should not assume everyone is racist with no evidence.

DEI initiatives are strategic actions that organizations take to promote diversity, equity, and inclusion (DEI) in the workplace. They stress hiring people based on perceived misrepresented groups rather than the ability or character of individuals. This is institutionalized prejudice. Diversity means to include groups according to race, cultures, or sex identity (but not according to ideological disagreements) and it excludes certain races. Equity is the idea that everyone has a right to the same things as everyone else whether or not they have earned it (communism). Inclusion is incorporating everyone into a group. Even though they try to sound like they include everyone, people with differing views or ideas are not welcome, as I personally experienced.

The solution to the opposition of trans children participating in sports is to have sports events specifically for them. No child is born in the wrong body. There are boys and there are girls and they are perfect. Gender affirming care, or transitioning medicine, for minors should be banned—it is child abuse. These are extreme medications and surgeries and a human being has the right to grow up and decide for themselves such a serious and permanent choice. Children don't have the maturity to make such irreversible decisions.

On their website in 2024, MSJ has a "Safe Schools Reading List." On

---

66. Montessori for Social Justice, *Montessori for Social Justice*.

67. Montessori for Social Justice, "2023 MSJ Conference: Imagining Liberation," *Montessori for Social Justice*, 2023.

this list, there are books about: gender, gender identity, and gendered society; transgenderism, sexuality, and love; pride, joy, and differences; bodies and consent; diverse fiction; drag queens; private colors; and pronouns. Here are a few samples of book titles by age:

- Children aged 0–3: *ABC Pride*; *Being You: A First Conversation about Gender*; *My Two Moms and Me*; and *Pronoun Book*.
- Children aged 3–6 are: *Gender Identity for Kids*; *I'm Not a Girl*; *Jacob's New Dress*; *Sam is my Sister*; *She's My Dad*; *The Gender Wheel*; *When Aiden Became a Brother*; *Two Grooms a Cake: The Story of America's First Gay Wedding*; and *Bodies are Cool*.
- Children aged 6–9: *A Girl Named Adam*; *Door by Door: How Sarah McBride Became America's First Openly Transgender*; *Beyond the Gender Binary*; *Queer Heroes: Meet LGBTQ Heroes From Past and Present*; and *The Every Body Book*.
- Children aged 9–12: *How to Save Queendom*; *My Trans Parent*; *Pride: An Inspirational History of the LGBTQIA+ Movement*.
- Children aged 12–15: *Queer Power*; *The Book of Pride: LGBTQ Heroes Who Changed the World*; *Let's Talk About it: The Teen's Guide to Sex, Relationships, and Being Human*; *Pride: The Celebration and the Struggle*. [68]

My response: On the book list, I didn't see anything about the Montessori principle of the individual being the basis of peace and respect for others. For the older children, there was nothing about reality being the basis of knowledge, order being a basis for logic, and nothing about choice making or independence. All topics on the list are inappropriate for children and are meant to turn normal children away from normalcy.

On the Montessori for Social Justice website, there is a webinar called "Creating Safe Schools for LGBTQIA+ Students, Staff, and Families." [69] The presenter was Elena Rosemond-Hoerr "she/her" who introduced herself as a "queer Montessorian," parent, school administrator, and a primary teacher. Elena introduced two other people one of whom was a toddler teacher and a "queer parent." Elena supports queer students and families and said her school is very open about it. If a student "comes

---

68. Elena Rosemond-Hoerr, "On-Demand Webinars: Creating Safe Schools," *Montessori for Social Justice*.

69. Ibid.

out," they have a plan for how to handle it, and the student is supported. A kindergartner had "come out" (transitioning) a few years ago.

From the webinar: The children are talked to in a gender-neutral way, "Some people have uteruses, and some people have penises," instead of, "Girls have uteruses, and boys have penises." She tells the children over and over again that you can't tell someone's gender by looking at their body. You have to ask them.

My response: Telling a child that he can't tell the difference between boys and girls based on their bodies is a confusing idea. Gender, as it is often used today, is the same as a person's biological sex and children make the distinctions between the sexes very early. The teacher has decided that gender is socially constructed instead of biologically determined, so she tells children to ask other children for their gender. The teacher is pushing a conclusion she has made onto the children at an age when they do not have enough knowledge to judge if human behavior is constructed by others. I think Montessori's words apply here.

> ... a development of the will would be impossible if, instead of allowing order and clarity to mature in the mind, we should seek to encumber it with chaotic ideas, or with stores of lessons learned by heart, and then prevent children from making decisions by deciding everything for them.[70]

From the webinar: The teachers have lots of conversations with children about sexual topics on a regular basis. Books are one of the main ways to introduce these subjects and get conversations going.

My response: They admit that teachers initiate these "conversations." Teachers should not be talking to children about sex. That is the parent's job. If the child asks the teacher a specific question, she should tell him to talk to his parents about it. Then the teacher should call the parents and tell them what their child asked.

By drawing constant attention to sex and private body parts, the children will conclude that a person's physical attributes matter the most. Focusing on physical attributes is shallow and superficial. The message is that a person's primary identity is their sexual orientation, instead of a private part of his identity. A person's true identity is reliant upon his mind because his independent thoughts reveal who he is.

---

70. Maria Montessori, *Spontaneous Activity in Education*, (Robert Bentley) 185.

From the webinar: They put up pride flags and related art in the classroom to indicate it is a safe place.

My response: "A safe place." What is done for the straight students? Anything? An American flag? The American flag represents the freedom of thought and lifestyle that they need. It includes all individuals. The pride flag only includes certain political groups, only certain individuals, and is therefore not inclusive.

From the webinar: The upper elementary and secondary children can form a rainbow club or a gender and sexuality alliance. They are not sexualizing children. They introduce these subjects with books where the characters are animals.

My response: Concentrating on sex and advocating forming sex clubs and alliances is most certainly sexualizing children. The children are learning that identities are centered on sex. Substituting cute animals for humans doesn't change the subject matter. In fact, it can be even more alluring, which they doubtless know and rely upon.

From the webinar: It is just as important for us to support children who are queer or who may be in the future as it is to teach the other students how to support them. The kids are ok, but the adults are not. It is very important for friends of those who are coming out to support them.

My response: "It is very important for friends of those who are coming out to support them." The opinions of others are more important than the child feeling secure in the choice he made that should have been based on reality.

From the webinar: The teachers have conversations with kids about gender identities and promote LGBT communities/lifestyles, but say that the kids need to figure out by themselves how they want their lives to be.

My response: The teachers are the ones pushing certain lifestyles by focusing on them with their books and all their conversations.

From the webinar: There is so much in our society that wants to put kids in gendered boxes.

My response: People freely choose their gender roles. Often these roles are biologically based, because we are limited by our actual genetic makeup, and these teachers are attempting to prevent children from making their own choices by putting them in *pre-chosen* boxes. What will happen to the straight, white male child who decides he doesn't like all of this heavy-handed sex discussion? Is he accepted?

Montessori Organizations That Promote Social Justice

From the webinar: A teacher said, "There are things that I choose to do that I know will piss people off and then there are things that I chose to do that I know that I could get away with it and people won't bat an eye at it, but it will have just as big of an impact."

My response: Which means some things are done explicitly to push for change and other things are done under the rug. Transparency is not always present; manipulative techniques are used.

From the webinar: If a child says to her that her mom says only boys and girls can get married, a teacher responds, "Well, that's not actually true. Any two adults can get married."

My response: Teachers are not the parents and should not be pushing an agenda on the child. In addition, the teacher is undermining parents who disagree.

CHAPTER 4
Conclusion

Stand Firm

To review, there are four requirements of reasoning ability: reality, order, free will, and intellectual independence. The first step is identifying reality. Now, think about kids like Joey, the four-year-old with big brown eyes who asked me if I had ever been a purse. Imagine what might happen when he enters a "progressive Montessori school" with his mind ready to be set in motion, ready to learn how to learn, his fragile mind ready to structure a method of thinking, as he is thrust into the hands of social justice teachers.

- <u>He is told that not only can he be a purse if he feels like it, he can identify as anything he wants, including a girl</u>. This is a violation of reality (this isn't true). Lying to a child or confusing him about reality interferes with his ability to think.
- <u>He is told that all people with white skin are racist</u>. This is a violation of reality (this isn't true) and free will (he is indoctrinated with determinism before he has the ability to understand it) and independence (he views himself and other people as collectives instead of individuals). Since he is white, this message is devastating to his view of himself, and he begins to feel sad and depressed. Racism thwarts his ability to use his will because he thinks the behavior of people depends on their race or sex. He will not view his classmates as individuals, he will react to them emotionally without thinking. The other children in class begin to distrust him because they think he is racist. If he were black, he would begin to doubt the friendship of his white classmates. He would begin to wonder if there is any point to trying to improve, since the world is racist and so much is stacked against him. He may begin to develop a "victim" mentality—blaming any discomfort or setback on his own skin color and the hatred from others for something he has no control over—leading to his own self-hatred and lack of motivation.

- Instead of allowing Joey, whether he's white or black, to learn about other people from his own observations and experience, the social justice teachers brainwash him with false generalizations about entire groups of people. He learns to rely on what he has been told, because he doesn't have enough knowledge to be able to think it through on his own.
- <u>He is not taught the truth about the founding of the United States</u>. Violation of reality (the facts of what happened) and order (the logic of cause and effect). Not knowing what happened in the past, he is ignorant and unable to evaluate anything in history.
- <u>A drag queen reads him a book about explicit sex acts</u>. Violation of reality (the truth about sex is not presented, it is portrayed as disgusting and casual) and order, the hierarchy of knowledge (children are not ready for sex physically, intellectually or emotionally). Joey doesn't understand what is said to him about sex, doesn't understand the ugliness that the drag queens are portraying about sex and is left with negative emotions. He concludes something is wrong with him since he doesn't understand it and develops a poor self-image. He becomes vulnerable to sexual abuse because all taboos are gone and now adults can freely approach him about it without causing alarm.
- <u>He hears a girl say she feels like a boy and the teacher tells her she can change her sex</u>. Violation of reality (this isn't true). Adults should never tell a child that he can change his sex because that is an outright lie. Just because someone "feels" he is the opposite sex does not mean he "is" the opposite sex. Supporting the notion that lies are facts will block the child's cognitive ability.
- <u>A teacher tells Joey to lie to his parents if they ask about the book that was read to him at school</u>. Violation of reality (teaching the child to fake reality). The teacher is teaching Joey to fake reality to separate him from his family so the school can take charge of him.
- <u>Joey asks the drag queen if he (the drag queen) is a boy or a girl and the drag queen says, "Why does it matter?"</u> Violation of reality (drag queen is confusing Joey on purpose). Joey is confused, especially since he is wondering if a person can be a purse.
- <u>Joey breaks lots of rules and is not corrected</u>. Violation of reality (no one can do whatever he wants no matter who or what he affects) and free will (he doesn't learn how to control himself).

Conclusion

Will all this mutilation of reality help Joey? No, not only will it not help him, it will confuse him badly. The risk is his mind will remain at the concrete, perceptual level of functioning or it will operate with floating abstractions separated from reality. Joey's thought process is not only held back, it is sabotaged, his reasoning abilities are stunted, and his independence is impaired.

It is imperative that adults stand firm with children about the nature of reality. Unless the child is clearly pretending during play, adults must adhere to the truth instead of sanctioning the child's fantasy. It is fine for someone to insist he be addressed according to reality (his real name), but not when he disregards reality (his imagined sex or any other whim such as a furry cat). If a child identifies as a furry cat, no adult should call that child by a cat name or allow that child to use a box instead of a toilet. Refusing to participate in the child's illusions does not mean the adult is disrespectful of the child. Respecting the child is all about respecting reality, because disregarding it is promoting mental illness as Montessori pointed out.

It is not hateful to disagree with addressing children as "they/them" or to refuse to accept transgenderism or furries as normal. Disagreement does not equal hate. Disagreement can be a very caring position. If a loved one or valued friend "came out" as a drug addict, it would not be helpful to say, "Wow, that's great! Congratulations!" Knowing that he was headed for disaster and a lifetime of misery, his self-destruction should not be encouraged. Instead, he should be encouraged to seek help. If a child "comes out" by telling a teacher that he "feels" like the opposite sex, that teacher should immediately contact the parents and let them handle it. If a child separates from reality by seriously claiming he is a cat, the teacher should not let him live in a fantasy world. The teacher should tell him he is not a cat and alert the parents.

Because of the intellectual corruption of much of today's educational establishment, every Montessori school faithful to the Montessori method should have an explicit policy in the school handbook stating that the school adheres to the Montessori philosophy and rejects progressive education, Freirean pedagogy, Critical Theory, Queer pedagogy, drag pedagogy, and anything else that contradicts the pedagogy of Maria Montessori. Any child attempting to fake reality by claiming to be an animal, the opposite sex, etc., will be told the truth and the parents will be informed.

Save Montessori

Marxist philosophy holds the populace must be loyal to the State and only to the State. Therefore, the child must be brainwashed to believe that he is determined by group status instead of his own individual thought process. He must be separated from reality so he can't think for himself and only repeats what the State tells him.

Communism seeks to destroy autonomy—every single form of it, and social justice is helping Marxists to achieve that goal. Social justice in Montessori is an embarrassment and a betrayal to the Montessori principle of independence. If we want to keep our children, culture, and country healthy and stable, we must reject all systems that eliminate intellectual independence and uphold authentic Montessori education.

After I was cancelled from speaking at the Montessori Center in the Rockies, I wrote to some major Montessori organizations expressing my concerns about Montessori turning political. I wrote to the Association Montessori International (AMI) and explained that Marxism is behind the social justice movement including the drag queen events. I sent them the link to my article that explains what is really going on with drag queen story hour, and then I wrote:

> The social justice movement is going to kill Montessori unless you stop it, and it needs to stop. Please find the courage to protect innocent children by standing up to this insanity. You are an organization representing Montessori. Set the standards of education instead of following the sheep. Don't betray Montessori's legacy, and most importantly, don't betray the children.

I suggested that they make a statement opposing social justice in Montessori. Social justice will kill Montessori because it is at war with reality and does not teach the child how to reason. Instead, it impedes reason through mindless political indoctrination. AMI, the organization whose purpose is to safeguard the integrity of the Montessori movement needs to take a stand.

The AMI website states that the purpose of Montessori education is to teach children how to think:

> An AMI Montessori education assists children to develop to their full human potential by helping them "learn how to think." What do thinking

children do when they grow up? They become successful, accomplished adults contributing to a better world.[1]

Is AMI protecting the integrity of Montessori's method when it does not take a stand against social justice? Is AMI promoting normalization or abnormality by remaining silent when schools hire "queer" teachers or invite drag queens to school? What about the teachers who are indoctrinating children with false history, like the Marxist 1619 project? What about the schools that are sabotaging the child's relationship with reality? Is it moral to lie to children by supporting the idea that they can change their sex? Is it okay for teachers to talk about sex with their students in secret? Is it okay to hide a real agenda from parents? Where are all the conferences and webinars about Montessori's real vision for peace—the normalization of the child? Where are the webinars about reality, independence, free will, and order? Have Montessorians deserted the woman, the genius, who discovered the secret of childhood?

The role of a parent and of a teacher is to protect the child from harm, teach him how to think and make good choices, identify reality, help him understand long-range consequences, and help him understand that his feelings are not superior to reason. Think about children like Joey, who comes to you with a question about reality and looks at you with innocent and trusting eyes. Do you really think it is permissible to betray his trust? To impede his thinking process? We would shudder if we saw a mother bird pluck the feathers from the wings of her young, then push them out of the nest to struggle for survival, yet that is what is being done to our children.[2]

Social justice will destroy Montessori because it not only ignores the principles of the Montessori Method, it damages children. It trains them to be racist by judging others according to group affiliation instead of their individual characters. It allows the child to "identify" however he wants and fills his mind with fantasies (girls can be boys, etc.) which is a vicious slap at reality. The child's need for order is not respected when he is exposed to subjects (sex) for which he is not intellectually ready. His will is not trained when he is pressured, with constant conversations and books, to agree with teachers who are obsessed with certain lifestyles. He will not normalize when queer pedagogy tries to make him

---

1. American Montessori Society, "Montessori Philosophy," *AMI/USA*, 2024.
2. This point was made by Ayn Rand in *Atlas Shrugged*.

abnormal. A child can hardly become an independent thinker under these circumstances.

Social justice is a political movement that aims to take down capitalism. It does not belong in Montessori. The purpose of Montessori is not to indoctrinate children with one political view. In Montessori's own words:

> *In any case, this is the scientific movement, which is taking shape, and it aims at building up some barrier against the ever-spreading evil and at prescribing some remedy for the confused and disoriented soul of man. Education must attach itself to this movement.*
>
> *Believe me – the attempts of the so-called modern education, which is simply trying to deliver the child from presumed repression, are not on the right path. To let the pupils do what they like, to abuse them with light occupations, to lead them back to an almost wild state, does not solve the problem. The question is not to deliver man from some bonds, but to reconstruct: a reconstruction requires the elaboration of a "science of the human spirit." It is a patient work, an endeavor based on research, to which thousands of people, dedicated to this aim, must contribute.*
>
> *Whoever works for this ideal must be actuated by a great ideal, much greater than those political ideals, which have promoted social improvements, which concern only the material life of some groups of men oppressed by injustice or misery. This ideal is universal in its scope. It aims at the deliverance of the whole of humanity. Much patient work I repeat, is needed along this road towards the freedom and "valorization" of mankind.*[3]
>
> ...
>
> <u>*Not in the service of any political or social creed should the teacher work*</u>, *but in the service of the complete human being, able to exercise in freedom, a self-disciplined will and judgement, unperverted by prejudice and undistorted by fear.*[4] *(Emphasis added.)*

It is clear. Montessori is an educational method, not a political program, and it needs to return to its original purpose. We must reject the activ-

---

3. Maria, Montessori, *The Formation of Man*, 14.
4. Maria Montessori, *To Educate the Human Potential*, 3.

ists who would make it political and remake our culture by destroying the normal.

Maria Montessori fled Italy, her homeland, when she discovered a dreadful truth about the politics in her country that she couldn't ignore, and it is very alarming that Montessori schools are succumbing to the ideology that Maria Montessori ran away from during WWII.

> By the time she saw the preschoolers she had trained wearing Fascist uniforms as teenagers, she could no longer deny the brutal realities of the regime and the hopelessness of combating it from within and she left.[5]

Here is the unreconcilable dichotomy that Montessori schools need to answer. What is the difference between Mussolini using Montessori trained children for his political purposes and the Queer Pedagogy activists using Montessori students for their political purposes?

The Montessori movement is at a crossing point. In these turbulent times, our future lies in the minds of our children. Montessori is the best educational system that teaches children how to think in an organized, logical, clear, consistent, integrated manner. The Montessori Method promotes independence, and when implemented correctly, is enormously and amazingly successful. It's essential for saving our children and our civilization from the mindless rot consuming it.

Montessorians should be leaders, not followers. We must have the courage to stand against what we know to be wrong. We must even stand alone if no one will stand with us. For the love of the child, the Montessori establishment must reverse course immediately. Teach children how to think. Save Montessori. Nothing could be more important for their future and ours.

---

5. Rita Kramer, *Maria Montessori: A Biography*, 329.

Appendix A

The Tale of the Pilgrims [1]

The tale of the Pilgrims who came to America to escape tyranny is a heroic and moving one. Most children have been told the basic story of Thanksgiving. Here are some more facts for your own information or that you may want to discuss with your child this holiday:

- When the Pilgrims left their homeland, their friends and family shed many tears of anguish because they knew they would never see each other again—ever.
- There were two ships that set out for America, the Speedwell and the Mayflower, but they had to return to England several times because the Speedwell sprang a leak and needed repair. After trying to fix it several times, they decided to set sail on the Mayflower alone and leave the Speedwell behind. That meant most of the passengers boarded the Mayflower, and it was even more crowded than before. When they finally sailed for good, they had already eaten all the food they had stored to get them through their first winter in America.
- The long trip on the ship was miserable. There were many storms and a lack of food and warmth. Many Pilgrims got sick and two died. One sailor made fun of those who got sick. He himself fell ill, died, and was thrown overboard. One Pilgrim fell overboard but was rescued. One baby, Oceanus Hopkins, was born during the voyage.
- The Pilgrims and the sailors detested each other and fought horrendously. The Pilgrims didn't like the rough language and crude ways of the sailors. The sailors thought the Pilgrims were sissies and thought they prayed too much. But by the time they arrived in America, they had developed a mutual respect for each other. The Pilgrims ended up admiring the competence the sailors displayed to get them across the ocean in what was an obviously dangerous trip. And the sailors ended up admiring the Pilgrims for their courage and tenacity in their quest for freedom in a new and scary world.

1. Charlotte Cushman, "The Tale of the Pilgrims," *American Thinker*, November 25, 2010.

- Once they arrived in America, the Pilgrims traveled up and down the coast looking for a place to settle. It was November and winter was upon them. They had no time to waste. Yet they argued and argued about the best place to stop before choosing a spot on the Massachusetts coast.
- Winter settled in and there wasn't time to build Plymouth settlement, so most of the Pilgrims slept on the ship.
- During their first winter, almost half of the Pilgrims died due to starvation and disease. They snuck the dead out at night to bury them. They didn't want the Indians to know that so many of them were dying, fearing that if the Indians knew, they would take advantage and attack them.
- As difficult as winter was, when the sailors took the Mayflower back to England in the spring, not a single Pilgrim went with them. Freedom meant that much to them.
- In the succeeding years, the Pilgrims made a very important discovery that led to their eventual success. While true that Squanto aided the Pilgrims in their quest for food, the real reason for their victory over starvation was this:

Perhaps Bradford's greatest achievement was his revision of the colony's economic organization in 1623. Spurred by hunger, the colonists had worked hard in the fields during their first year, but in succeeding years it became more and more difficult to get them to put their best efforts into this essential task. Bradford decided that the reason was the stipulation in their contract with the London merchants that everything in the colony, including the crops, was to be held in common for seven years. This crude communism was crippling individual enterprise. Boldly, on his own authority, Bradford abandoned the arrangement and announced that henceforth every family would raise its own corn. Plymouth never went hungry again.

Life wasn't always easy. Our way of life in our country came about because of the painful suffering people were willing to endure in order to have freedom from tyranny. The lesson we and our children can learn from the Thanksgiving story is beautifully expressed by the first governor of Plymouth. William Bradford wrote in his diary:

As one small candle may light a thousand, so the light kindled here has shown unto many, yea in some sort to our whole nation.... We have noted these things so that you might see their worth and not negligently lose what your fathers have obtained with so much hardship.

Appendix B

Save Western Civilization—Defend Christopher Columbus [1]

When I taught, every October my students learned the story of Christopher Columbus. We started with what the world was like when he was alive. At that time, the Atlantic Ocean was called the Sea of Darkness because many people still believed that huge dangerous sea-dragons lived there ready to feast on and swallow up any ship that ventured into its waters. In addition, many people thought the ocean flowed downhill so that even if you could get past the dragons, your ship would eventually slide so far down that it couldn't get back up. The sea was a dangerous and terrifying place. Sailors were scared to sail in the Sea of Darkness.

Then along came Christopher Columbus. He was a sailor looking for a shorter way to travel to Asia. He was scientifically oriented and was convinced that the world was really round, like other men were speculating, and that he should be able to find his shortcut. He eventually convinced Queen Isabella and King Ferdinand to fund and support his mission. He was able to acquire three ships and sailed west with his crew to reach the Indies.

They sailed on and on and on and on and they didn't find land. Two months went by. His crew got impatient and angry and were considering mutiny. They demanded he turn the ship and go home, but Columbus refused. Two days later, on October 12, they found land and Columbus was elated—he thought he'd found his shortcut. Little did he know that he had discovered a whole new continent and, sadly, he carried this unawareness with him to his death.

The students learn that Columbus' discovery of America led to the age of exploration. Other sailors and explorers wanted to know what was in the wider world and set out on great adventures across the sea. This led to the colonization of far-off lands and ultimately the creation of the United States of America. Later, they learn that the United States was the first country to recognize individual rights and therefore people

---

1. Charlotte Cushman, "Save Western Civilization," *American Thinker,* October 10, 2011.

of all races could live in harmony. This new recognition of rights also gave everyone the freedom to pursue his own interests. That freedom led to inventions such as the light bulb, airplane, phonograph, telephone, refrigerator, washing machine, dish washer, modern medical procedures, and so on. For the first time, enormous happiness was possible to people. People could also create widespread wealth.

It is important that children know this story. Why? Because it is their story, a story about Western Civilization which is their heritage. They need to know the events that led to the founding of their country. They need to know that the United States didn't always have cars, televisions, computers, stores, and enough food to eat, and then learn how it came to be that we have all these things. They also need to understand human virtues such as courage, reason and strength of character and what can happen when someone exercises his own judgment in the face of opposition. In essence, what they need to understand is consequences, that there are reasons why things happen and that they need to pay attention to those reasons. Children used to be taught this story in our schools years ago.

Then along came multiculturalism. Most people think that multiculturalism is just about learning interesting things about other cultures, such as that the Japanese wear kimonos and the Mexicans eat tacos, but multiculturalism as a doctrine goes much deeper than that. It holds that all cultures, no matter what their nature, are morally equal. I disagree. Would you say that no individual is morally better than any other? A scientist working on a cure for cancer is no better than a mass murderer? Hardly. One is working to extend life, the other to extinguish it. Cultures should be judged the same way. Some encourage life to flourish, others don't. Western Civilization enhances man's life and happiness. Traveling by automobile or airplane is better than drifting on rafts; creating medical cures is better than chanting and prancing around a fire; living in warm, cozy homes during the winter is better than shivering and suffering in the frigid forest. All cultures are not the same. And since multiculturalism denies that fact, it seeks to obliterate the story of Columbus because he is an integral part of the history of Western Civilization. (There are even movements that do away with Columbus Day altogether and condemn industrial civilization outright.) [2]

---

2. Red-Coral.net, "Berkeley Indigenous Peoples Day: Pow Wow & Indian Market," *red-coral.net*, 2008.

Here are a few of the contrived attacks that have been flung against Columbus and a refutation of each.

- "Columbus didn't really discover America since people already lived here." Yes, he did, for Europe. The people in Europe didn't know the American continent was there, and his discovery affected their perception of the world and inspired the discoveries Europeans made thereafter. Look at it this way, if we go to a planet in outer space and find that there are people living there, does that mean we didn't discover that planet because… people were already living there? What kind of logic is that?
- "Columbus inaugurated an era of slavery." No, he didn't. Slavery was common throughout the world at that time.
- "Columbus and the Europeans took away land that belonged to the Indians." The Indians never stayed in any one place to develop and own any land. They were constantly roaming all over the country. In addition, since there was no concept of land ownership, it couldn't be taken away.
- "The Indians were just peaceful people." No, most weren't. While there were some exceptions to this (Pocahontas and Sacagawea), most of them were killing and slaughtering each other years before the white man came. They pretty much lived in a constant state of war.
- "Columbus himself took personal leadership in acts that would today be called genocide."[3] We cannot judge people in history by the standards that we have at present. Just as we cannot criticize the Indians for failing to understand that there were no spirits that lived in human hair (which is why they scalped people), we cannot criticize the Europeans for failing to understand individual rights. The concept of individual rights did not yet exist. It is true that gruesome incidents took place which cannot be condoned, but this was no different from the way Europeans treated other Europeans and the way Indians treated other Indians.
- "The Indians lived in harmony with the earth." Multi-culturalists would have us believe that the Indians were always happy and carefree, as if they were tiptoeing through the forest throwing tulip petals along the way. The truth is that because they did not understand science and

---

3. Red-Coral.net, "Berkeley Indigenous Peoples Day: Pow Wow & Indian Market," *red-coral.net*, 2008.

natural law, it was very difficult for them to survive as they suffered famine, disease, drought, floods, and malnutrition. They weren't as happy as we are led to believe—they often felt afraid and helpless. Besides, running herds of buffalo off cliffs only to use a few of them and leaving the rest to rot is not "living in harmony with the earth."

- "Columbus and the Europeans are to blame for introducing diseases such as smallpox, which killed many Indians." This is absurd on the face of it. Can you imagine Europeans sitting around plotting about what disease they could get next so that they could give it to the Indians? Not to mention that during the 15th, 16th, and 17th centuries, people had no idea what caused diseases. That knowledge came with science. Using the same line of reasoning, perhaps we should blame the Indians for introducing the Europeans to tobacco because smokers have died of lung cancer.

Have you ever wondered why Christopher Columbus is under attack? It is because he symbolizes the beginning of America, which is a shining product of Western Civilization. But if no culture is supposed to be morally superior to any other, then why is Western Civilization under assault? Which culture is attacking it and from what moral platform? And why is it that an American child is supposed to learn about every culture except his own? Those are contradictions that multiculturalists don't answer.

When Columbus is viciously condemned, it is the dominant ideas of our culture that are threatened. Reason, science, individualism, and progress *are* morally superior to collectivism and stagnation. The ideas of Western Civilization have led to our survival, well-being, and happiness. Let's not return to the Sea of Darkness. It is time to stand up and defend Christopher Columbus.

Appendix C

The Unknown Story of Pocahontas [1]

One of the most remarkable stories is the story of Pocahontas who died over 400 years ago on March 21, 1617. She, along with the leadership of Captain John Smith, was instrumental in the success of Jamestown, the first English colony to survive in America. Children today are pretty unaware of what really happened. The only real exposure they have is typically from the Walt Disney movie, Pocahontas, where the story is totally distorted.

In the Walt Disney film, the Europeans are portrayed as evil, coming to the New World only in search of gold and the desire to kill Indians. The Indians, on the other hand, are all portrayed as benevolent and good, living simply and peacefully. Chief Powhatan is portrayed as wise and kindly, but he has betrothed his daughter, Pocahontas, to Kocoum, whom she doesn't wish to marry. When Pocahontas meets Captain John Smith, they fall in love, but she finds fault with him for being racist and lectures him with a song. Later, while the Englishmen are out hoping to annihilate the Indians and confiscate their gold, Kocoum attacks Captain John Smith and is killed by another Englishman. Thinking that Smith killed Kocoum, he is captured and sentenced to die. The audience is then treated to a song called "Savages." The Englishmen sing, "Here's what you get when races are diverse. Their skin's a hellish red. They're only good when dead." The Indians sing this as they prepare for battle: "The paleface is a demon. The only thing they feel at all is greed." The English are portrayed as being motivated by prejudice and greed, but the Indians' fury is mitigated by a misunderstanding.

Pocahontas resolves to stop the war and as Smith is about to be killed, she throws herself upon him as the axe is about to fall. Her father, touched by her love for Smith, calls off his warriors and the English soldiers reciprocate. The governor of the English, Ratcliffe, however, grabs a gun and tries to shoot Powhatan when Smith throws himself

---

1. Charlotte Cushman, "The Unknown Story of Pocahontas, *American Thinker*, May 14, 2011.

in front of the chief and is seriously wounded. He and Pocahontas tearfully separate as his only hope for recovery lies in returning to London for treatment.

Now let's look at what really happened. First of all, the English settlers came to America in search of freedom, not because they wanted to kill Indians and steal their gold. Freedom was so important to the settlers that they endured many hardships and suffering such as fire, drought, Indian attacks, disease, starvation and death, which wiped out half the colony. (The movie doesn't even acknowledge this.)

The Indians, on the other hand, were, for the most part, uncivilized and roamed the countryside warring with each other and other tribes. They tortured and murdered prisoners with ceremonial dancing and feasts, scalped strangers, and annually sacrificed 2–3 children chosen by witch doctors. They were doing this before white men ever appeared on the shore.

Pocahontas was 10 years old when the English came to settle at Jamestown. She was a happy child and was often laughing, singing, and playing. She played with the young cabin boys and studied the tools they used. She was filled with wonder and admiration at what these strangers had accomplished as they were more advanced than her own people. She was especially fascinated with the axe and what the colonists could do with it to make buildings. Pocahontas became friends with the settlers and learned their language and everyone's name that first summer. She especially liked Captain John Smith (who was married and 27 years old) and by Fall began to teach him her language. She brought food to the colonists and warned them of Indian attacks.

Chief Powhatan, father to Pocahontas, did not share her admiration for the Englishmen. That winter when Smith was on a map making expedition, the Indians captured him and condemned him to death. Powhatan was not so wise and kindly (as the movie wants us to believe) otherwise Pocahontas would have been able to reason with him. Instead, she had to stand against her very own father and her people to save Smith's life. In Smith's own words, "At the minute of my execution, she hazarded the beating of her own brains to save mine."

After that, Chief Powhatan used Pocahontas (now age 11) as an emissary to the colony. Without her, Jamestown probably would have disappeared like Roanoke Colony before them. In the meantime, Smith was injured in a gun powder accident (he was not shot by Ratcliff) and sent back to London to recover. In 1608, Powhatan was angered by the Colonists' wish to seek peace with him so he threatened Pocahontas with death if she continued to help the Colonists. She did anyway.

In 1609, it was a terrible winter and the Colonists were starving. The Indians were preparing to attack them, so Powhatan sent Pocahontas to a faraway village.

In 1613, the Colonists decided to kidnap some Indians to get Chief Powhatan to negotiate with them. Pocahontas (now 15 or 16) was lured on a boat near modern-day Washington, D.C., and brought to Jamestown where she was met as a heroine, much to the surprise of those who brought her there. Chief Powhatan was indifferent to the fact they had his daughter.

Next, Pocahontas went to John Rolfe's tobacco plantation to teach him her knowledge of tobacco. While there, she also studied Christianity, converted and was baptized Rebecca. In 1614, she married John Rolfe.

Two years later, Rolfe, Pocahontas, and their son, Thomas, plus 12 Indians went to England where she was received as a lady and was presented to Queen Anne as "Lady Rebecca of Virginia." While preparing to return to America, she gcontracted smallpox and died. She was buried in England with this plaque, "Rebecca Rolfe of Virginia, Lady Born." There is a statue of her there and a copy of it is in Jamestown. John Rolfe returned to Jamestown to build up his plantation and was killed by Pocahontas' uncle in 1622. Their son, Thomas, returned to America in 1635, married and had 12 children. These descendants married into Virginia families and some eventually served in the United States Senate and House of Representatives.

Unlike the Walt Disney movie, the real story of Pocahontas demonstrates the triumph of individualism over racism. If the English considered Indians to be racially inferior, or if the English were true racists, the honorable tribute to Pocahontas in England and Virginia would never have been erected, nor would her descendants have ever been elected to the U.S. government.

Pocahontas is the tale of a heroine, a child who exhibited moral courage and independence, a child who went against everything she'd been taught all her life in favor of the convictions of her own mind, thus proving that one's race does not have to determine one's culture or destiny. Her bravery was a great and crucial help to the survival of the colony at Jamestown, and she deserves to be remembered as a part of our country's legacy. Our children should not be denied the joy of knowing the real story of Pocahontas. They deserve to feel pride in their American heritage—that of freedom, courage and individualism.

Bibliography

Alfonseca, Kiara. "Florida House passes controversial 'Don't Say Gay' bill." *ABC News*. February 24, 2022. Accessed April 17, 2024. https://abcnews.go.com/Politics/florida-house-passes-controversial-dont-gay-bill/story?id=83090590.

American Montessori Society. "AMS Affinity Groups: Safe, brave, and inclusive environments for our members." *AMS*. Accessed April 30, 2024. https://amshq.org/Educators/Community/AMS-Affinity-Groups.

American Montessori Society. "Anti-bias, Antiracist (ABAR) Certificate Program." *AMS*. Accessed April 27, 2024. https://learn.amshq.org/abar-certificate-program.

American Montessori Society. "Election Results: AMS Board of Directors." *AMS*. June 4, 2020. Accessed May 7, 2024. https://amshq.org/Educators/Community/Announcements/All-Announcements/2020/2020-05-22-Election-Results-AMS-Board-of-Directors.

American Montessori Society. "Equity Examined Workshop." *AMS*. August 15 and 22, 2024. Accessed May 14, 2024. https://amshq.org/Educators/Community/Special-Publications/Equity-Examined-Workshop.

American Montessori Society. "History of the American Montessori Society." *AMS*. Accessed April 28, 2024. https://amshq.org/About-AMS/History-of-AMS.

American Montessori Society. "The Mission of the American Montessori Society: Empowering humanity to build a better world through Montessori." *AMS*. Accessed July 29, 2024. https://amshq.org/About-AMS/What-is-AMS.

American Montessori Society. "Montessori Philosophy." *AMI/USA*. 2024. Accessed April 17, 2024. https://amiusa.org/about/montessori-philosophy.

AMI/USA. "AMI/USA Equity Statement." *AMI/USA*. February 11, 2021. Accessed April 28, 2024. https://mcusercontent.com/20a529440a756f6e7049e35b0/files/c4532d45-271a-4c57-a206-2f67aaebf1fc/Final_Equity_Statement_021121.pdf.

AMI/USA. "Keynote Address from Gretchen Hall." *AMI/USA*. February 20, 2018. Accessed May 3, 2024. https://amiusa.org/news/keynote-address-from-gretchen-hall.

AMI/USA. "Montessori for Social Justice Conference." *AMI/USA*. May 7, 2018. Accessed May 20, 2024. https://amiusa.org/news/montessori-for-social-justice-conference.

AMI/USA. "National Day of Mourning." *Facebook: AMI/USA*. November 24, 2022. Accessed April 17, 2024. https://www.facebook.com/AMIUSA/posts/pfbid0BZwagCBdoUZ1stuxno7yTVCa42JzwvNMKyd1BCYz2UiZXYpKtqGGQx5QaKS5cuHhl?comment_id=1455062521668234&notif_id=1669313441170600&notif_t=feed_comment_reply&ref=notif.

AMI/USA. "Refresher Course Workshops." *AMI/USA*. September 12, 2017. Accessed April 27, 2024. https://amiusa.org/news/refresher-course-workshops.

AMI/USA. "Social Justice Webinar Series." *AMI/USA*. September 8, 2020. Accessed April 28, 2024. https://amiusa.org/news/social-justice-webinar-series.

Ayer, David. "Montessori For Social Justice." *National Center for Montessori in the Public Sector*. May 23, 2016. Accessed May 23, 2016. https://www.montessoripublic.org/2016/05/montessori-for-social-justice.

Banks, Kira and R. Alex Maixner. "Social Justice Education in an Urban Charter Montessori School." *Journal of Montessori Research* 2, no. 2 (2016). Accessed April 28, 2024. https://journals.ku.edu/jmr/article/view/5066.

Bavard, Rachel. "Government dictating what social-media bans is tyrannical." *New York Post*. July 16, 2021. Accessed July 28, 2024. https://nypost.com/2021/07/16/government-dictating-what-social-media-bans-is-tyrannical.

Berliner, Michael and Harry Binswanger. "Answers to Common Questions about Montessori Education." *The Objectivist Forum* 5 (June & August 1984).

Berliner, Michael. "Montessori and Social Development." *The Educational Forum* (March, 1974).

Berliner, Michael. "Reason, Creativity and Freedom in Montessori." *The Educational Forum* (November, 1975).

Betzold, Todd. "Convicted murderer released from prison, allegedly kills again weeks later after smoking 'speed'." *Front Page Detectives*. November 18, 2021. Accessed September 30, 2024. https://www.frontpagedetectives.com/p/texas-convicted-murderer-kills-again.

Bezmenov, Yuri. "Yuri Bezmenov - How To Demoralize A Nation." *YouTube*. June 21, 2020. Accessed May 3, 2024. https://www.youtube.com/watch?v=Hr5sTGxMUdo.

Binswanger, Harry. "Logical Thinking." July 1–7, 1992, paper presented at Objectivist conference, Williamsburg, Virginia.

Bishop, Sheri. "Preparing Ourselves Spiritually and Mentally for Revolutionary Social Change." *AMI/USA*. November 20, 2015. Accessed May 17, 2024. https://amiusa.org/event/preparing-ourselves-spiritually-and-mentally-for-revolutionary-social-change.

Bishop, Sheri. "Racial Equity: An Important Call to Action for Administrators and Board of Directors." *AMI/USA*. February 24, 2021. Accessed July 29, 2024. https://amiusa.org/sheri-bishop-february-24-2021.

Bloomberg, Sara. "Exploring Gender Expansiveness in the Montessori Environment." *AMI/USA*. March 20, 2023. Accessed May 17, 2024. https://amiusa.org/event/exploring-gender-expansiveness-in-the-montessori-environment.

Bloomberg, Sara interviewed by The Male Montessorian. May 31, 2019. "The Queer Montessorian: an interview with Sara Bloomberg." *The Male Montessorian*. Accessed May 7, 2024. http://themalemontessorian.com/2019/05/31/the-queer-montessorian-an-interview-with-sara-bloomberg.

Bloomberg, Sara interviewed by West Side Montessori. *West Side Montessori School*. Accessed May 7, 2024. https://wsmsnyc.org/teachereducation/sara-bloomberg.

Bowden, Thomas. *The Enemies of Christopher Columbus*. New Jersey: Paper Tiger, 2007.

Bradley, Michael. *Yes, Your Teen is Crazy*. Port Charlotte, Florida: Harbor Press, 2003.

Briggs, Dorothy. "Self-esteem." Spring 1982, paper presented at workshop, Tacoma, Washington.

Brown, Siobhan Growing Elm. "Gratitude for The National Day of Mourning." *AMI/USA*. November 24, 2022. Accessed April 17, 2024. https://amiusa.org/news/gratitude-for-the-national-day-of-mourning.

California State Department of Education. "Caught in the middle: Educational reform for young adolescents in California public school." 1987.

Calvin, Donna. "The 45 Communist Goals as read into the congressional record." *BeliefNet.* January 10, 1963. Accessed April 28, 2024. https://www.beliefnet.com/columnists/watchwomanonthewall/2011/04/the-45-communist-goals-as-read-into-the-congressional-record-1963.html.

CBS News. "Florida Governor DeSantis defends controversial "Don't Say Gay" bill." *CBS News.* March 5, 2022. Accessed April 17, 2024. https://www.cbsnews.com/news/florida-governor-desantis-defends-dont-say-gay-bill.

CBS News. "Minneapolis police precinct and businesses set on fire as protests over George Floyd's death rage on." *CBS News.* May 29, 2020. https://www.cbsnews.com/news/george-floyd-protests-minneapolis-police-third-precinct. *USSA News.* August 27, 2020. https://ussanews.com/News1/2020/08/27/portland-mayor-ted-wheeler-proposed-ordering-police-to-stand-down-during-antifa-riots.

Child Welfare Information Gateway. "Child Abuse and Neglect." *ChildWelfare.org.* Accessed April 17, 2024. https://www.childwelfare.gov/topics/safety-and-risk/child-abuse-and-neglect.

Chitwood, Deb. "Best Maria Montessori Quotes." *Bits of Positivity* (blog). January 10, 2017. Accessed May 17, 2024. https://bitsofpositivity.com/best-maria-montessori-quotes.

Coe, Elizabeth Johnston. "Montessori and the Middle School Years." *Montessori and Contemporary Social Problems*, circa 1985.

Coloroso, Barbara. *Kids are Worth It: Giving Your Child the Gift of Inner Discipline.* New York: Harper Collins Publishers, 1994.

Congressional Record. *Congressional Record — House.* US Congress, January 10, 1963. Accessed April 16, 2024. https://www.congress.gov/88/crecb/1963/01/10/GPO-CRECB-1963-pt1-2-1.pdf.

Cullors, Patricia. "BLM Co-Founder Patrisse Cullors 'We are Marxists, we (sic) are Ideological'." *YouTube*, June 19, 2020. https://www.youtube.com/watch?v=Pyhy4IvkENg.

Cullors, Patrisse interviewed with Martyn Iles. "We Are Trained Marxists." June 19, 2020. *YouTube.* Accessed April 26, 2024. https://www.youtube.com/watch?v=HgEUbSzOTZ8.

Cushman, Charlotte. "After Drag Queens, Pedophilia is Next." *American Thinker.* June 18, 2022. Accessed April 17, 2024. https://www.

americanthinker.com/blog/2022/06/after_drag_queens_pedophilia_is_next.html.

Cushman, Charlotte. "Montessori Organization Debunks Thanksgiving." *American Thinker.* November 27, 2022. Accessed April 17, 2024. https://www.americanthinker.com/blog/2022/11/_montessori_organization_debunks_thanksgiving_story_.html.

Cushman, Charlotte. "Montessori Teacher Fights 'Social Justice'." *American Thinker.* March 12, 2022. https://www.americanthinker.com/articles/2022/03/montessori_teacher_fights_social_justice.html.

Cushman, Charlotte. "Montessori Teacher Fights 'Social Justice'." *Capitalism Magazine.* March 14, 2022. https://www.capitalismmagazine.com/2022/03/montessori-teacher-fights-social-justice.

Cushman, Charlotte. "The Real Purpose of Drag Queen Story Hour." *American Thinker.* January 21, 2023. https://www.americanthinker.com/articles/2023/01/the_real_purpose_of_drag_queen_story_hour.html.

Cushman, Charlotte. "The Real Purpose of Drag Queen Story Hour: The purpose is to turn children "queer" through an educational process." *Capitalism Magazine.* January 22, 2023. https://www.capitalismmagazine.com/2023/01/the-real-purpose-of-drag-queen-story-hour.

Cushman, Charlotte. "Save Western Civilization, Defend Christopher Columbus." *American Thinker.* October 10, 2011. Accessed April 17, 2024. https://www.americanthinker.com/articles/2011/10/save_western_civilization_defend_christopher_columbus.html.

Cushman, Charlotte. "The Tale of the Pilgrims, Why It Needs to Be Taught." *American Thinker.* November 25, 2010. Accessed April 17, 2024. https://www.americanthinker.com/articles/2010/11/the_tale_of_the_pilgrims_why_i.html.

Cushman, Charlotte. "The Unknown Story of Pocahontas." *American Thinker.* May 14, 2011. Accessed April 17, 2024. https://www.americanthinker.com/articles/2011/05/the_unknown_story_of_pocahonta.html.

Cushman, Charlotte. "Yes, Transgender Transformation is Child Abuse." *American Thinker*, June 16, 2022. Accessed April 17, 2024. https://www.americanthinker.com/blog/2022/06/yes_transgender_transformation_is_child_abuse.html.

Davis, Jack. "Shortly After Targeting Conservative Media, FBI Raids Home of Republican Election Official." *Western Journal.* November

21, 2021. https://www.westernjournal.com/shortly-targeting-conservative-media-fbi-raids-home-republican-election-official.

Dennis, Chad. "Black Montessori Education Fund Anniversary Fundraiser." *Black Montessori Education Fund on Eventbrite*. July 30, 2021. Accessed May 17, 2024. https://www.eventbrite.com/x/black-montessori-education-fund-anniversary-fundraiser-tickets-163273554597.

Dewey, John. *Democracy and Education*. New York: The Macmillan Company, 1916. Accessed October 25, 2024. https://archive.org/details/democracyandeduc00deweuoft/page/n159/mode/2up.

Dewey, John. "Human Nature and Conduct." *Internet Archive*. New York: The Modern Library, 1930. Accessed October 25, 2024. https://archive.org/details/in.ernet.dli.2015.213957.

Dewey, John. "My Pedagogic Creed." *School Journal* 54 (January 1897).

Dewey, John. "The Primary-Education Fetich." *The Forum 1898-05* 25, no. 3. Open Court Publishing Co.. Accessed April 23, 2024. https://archive.org/details/sim_forum-and-century_1898-05_25_3/page/314/mode/2up.

Dewey, John. *The Quest for Certainty*. New York: G.P. Putnam's Sons, 1960.

Dewey, John. "Reconstruction in Philosophy." Freeditorial.com. August 4, 2014. Accessed July 28, 2024. https://freeditorial.com/en/books/reconstruction-in-philosophy.

Dewey, John. Reconstruction in Philosophy. New York: H. Holt, 1920. Accessed October 25, 2024. https://archive.org/details/reconstructionin00deweuoft/page/94/mode/2up?q=construct.

Dewey, John. "The Relation of Theory to Practice in Education." People.ucsc.edu. Accessed October 25, 2024. https://people.ucsc.edu/~ktellez/dewey_relation.pdf.

Dewey, John. "The School and Social Progress." The School and Society. Chicago: University of Chicago Press, 1907.

Di Angelo, Robin. White Fragility. Boston: Beacon Press, 2018. Accessed April 17, 2024. https://www.amazon.com/White-Fragility-People-About-Racism-ebook/dp/B07638ZFN1/ref=tmm_kin_swatch_0?_encoding=UTF8&sr=1-1.

Dictionary.com. "Free will." Dictionary.com. 2024. Accessed April 18, 2024. https://www.dictionary.com/browse/free-will.

Doezema, Marie. "France, Where Age of Consent Is Up for Debate." The Atlantic. March 10, 2008. Accessed April 17, 2024. https://www.

theatlantic.com/international/archive/2018/03/frances-existential-crisis-over-sexual-harassment-laws/550700.

Drag Story Hour NYC. "Events: Program Partners." Drag Story Hour NYC. Accessed June 22, 2024. https://www.dshnyc.org/events.

Dreikurs, Rudolf. Children: the Challenge. New York: Plume, 1987. http://www.newworldencyclopedia.org/entry/Rudolf_Dreikurs.

Durden, Tyler. "Texas AG Urges Prosecution Over "Grotesque" 'Child-Friendly' Drag Show Near Dallas." Zero Hedge. October 19, 2022. Accessed 2022. https://www.zerohedge.com/political/texas-ag-urges-prosecution-over-horrific-child-friendly-drag-show-near-dallas.

E (@ElijahSchaffer). "INSANE: Furries take over a public school Students protest and claim they are being bitten That there are litter boxes in the bathrooms WHAT IS GOING ON IN PUBLIC SCHOOLS?" X.com. April 19, 2024. https://x.com/ElijahSchaffer/status/1781300549226463504.

Edgemont Montessori School. "Restorative Justice." Edgemont Montessori School. 2024. Accessed September 30, 2024. https://edgemont.montclair.k12.nj.us/about_our_school/restorative_justice.

End Wokeness (@EndWokenes). "LEGO just released a LGBTQ+ Pride video with furries and drag queens marching:" X.com. June 20, 2024. https://x.com/EndWokeness/status/1803849139656233307.

End Wokeness (@EndWokenes). "What a time to be alive. Yesterday, over 70 students walked out of Mt. Nebo School to protest the school for letting "furries" to bite, bark, & lick them." X.com. April 18 2024. https://x.com/EndWokeness/status/1780985197741121691.

"FBI charges multiple individuals for peaceful protests at abortion facility." Live Action. October 5, 2022. https://www.liveaction.org/news/fbi-charges-multiple-individuals-peaceful-protests-abortion.

Fenny, Sam. "Texas AG Urges Prosecution Over 'Grotesque' 'Child-Friendly' Drag Show Near Dallas." David Icke. October 21, 2022. Accessed September 30, 2024. https://davidicke.com/2022/10/21/texas-ag-urges-prosecution-over-grotesque-child-friendly-drag-show-near-dallas.

Fleming, Thomas. One Small Candle. New York: W. W. Norton and Company, 1964.

Foreman, Jonathan. "The truth Johnny Depp wants to hide about the real-life Tontos: How Comanche Indians butchered babies, roasted enemies alive and would ride 1,000 miles to wipe out one family." The

Daily Mail. August 18, 2013. Accessed April 17, 2024. https://www.dailymail.co.uk/news/article-2396760/How-Comanche-Indians-butchered-babies-roasted-enemies-alive.html.

Foucault, Michel. "The Danger of Child Sexuality." Uib.no. April 4, 1978. Accessed September 18, 2024. https://www.uib.no/sites/w3.uib.no/files/attachments/foucaultdangerchildsexuality_0.pdf.

Gates, Bill. "Bill Gates - Population – Vaccines." *YouTube*. December 9, 2010. https://www.youtube.com/watch?v=DtkfWaCzsas.

Gates, Katherine. "Furries." *Deviant Desires: Incredibly Strange Sex*. New York: Juno Books, 1999. Accessed September 19, 2024 from *encyclopedia.com*. https://www.encyclopedia.com/social-sciences/encyclopedias-almanacs-transcripts-and-maps/furries.

Gays Against Groomers (@againstgrmrs). "The furries are out of hand. There is no pride in parading around your fetish in the street, especially in front of children. Somebody call animal control." *X.com*. August 28, 2024. https://x.com/againstgrmrs/status/1828800023775355349.

George, Marilyn. "Two and-Three-Year Olds" and "Four, Five and Six-Year Olds." *Blue Gables Montessori School, Kirkland, Washington*.

Ginott, Haim. *Between Parent and Child*. New York: MacMillan Company, 1965.

Glenn, Stephen and Jane Nelson. *Raising Self-Reliant Children*. Rocklin, California: Prima Publishing, 1980.

Goehring, Charles. "Gender Diversity and Inclusivity in the Classroom." *AMS*. Summer 2017. https://amshq.org/About-Montessori/Montessori-Articles/All-Articles/Gender-Diversity-and-Inclusivity-in-the-Classroom.

Gordon, Thomas. *Parent Effectiveness Training*. New York: Peter H. Wyden Inc., 1970.

Goudsmit, Linda. *Space Is No Longer the Final Frontier–Reality Is*. St. Pete Beach, Florida: Contrapoint Publishing, 2024.

Graber, David. "Mother Nature as a Hothouse Flower: The End of Nature." *Los Angeles Times*. October 22, 1989. https://www.latimes.com/archives/la-xpm-1989-10-22-bk-726-story.html, (accessed September 30, 2024).

Greater Haverhill Chamber. "June Art Walk celebrates pride with drag queens and more!" *Greater Haverhill Chamber*. Accessed June 23, 2024. https://www.haverhillchamber.com/member-news/june-art-walk-celebrates-pride-with-drag-queens-and-more.

Bibliography

Great River School. "January 2022 GRS Board Updates." *GreatRiverSchool.org*. February 2, 2022. Accessed July 28, 2024. https://www.greatriverschool.org/newsletter/2022/2/2/january-2022-grs-board-updates?rq=restorative%20justice.

Greenspring Montessori School. "Diversity, Equity, Inclusion, and Belonging, at Greenspring Montessori School." *Green Spring Montessori*. Accessed May 25, 2024. https://greenspringmontessori.org/diversity-equity-inclusion-belonging.

Grossman, Mariam testifies to US House Committee. "She Destroys Gender Ideology in 5 Minutes." *YouTube*. August 10, 2023. Accessed May 5, 2024. https://www.youtube.com/watch?v=abTMFKoytMo.

Han, Daisy and Trisha Moquino. "Moving Beyond Peace Education to Social Justice Education." *AMI/USA Journal* (Spring 2018). Accessed September 23, 2024. https://peacemaking.narf.org/wp-content/uploads/2021/04/MovingBeyondPeaceEducationtoSocialJustice-Education.pdf

Hanford, Emily. "At a Loss for Words." *APM News Report*, August 22, 2019. Accessed July 28, 2024. https://www.apmreports.org/episode/2019/08/22/whats-wrong-how-schools-teach-reading.

Healy, Jane. *Endangered Minds: Why Children Don't Think and What We Can Do About It*. New York: Simon and Schuster, 1990.

Healy, Jane. *Your Child's Growing Mind: A Guide to Learning and Brain Development from Birth to Adolescence*. New York: Broadway Books, 2004.

Healy, Jane. "An Interview with Jane Healy." *Wild Duck Review* IV, no. 2 (1998).

Heartland Signal (@HeartlandSignal). "Nebraska State Sen. Bostelman (R) falsely says that school children are being encouraged to identify as cats: "If you don't know what furries are, it's when kids dress up as cats or dogs, during the school day... Schools are wanting to put litter boxes in... for kids to use."" *X.com*. March 28, 2022. https://x.com/HeartlandSignal/status/1508506135212474376.

The Historian. "Black Slave Owners – 10 Most Famous." *Have Fun with History*. December 22, 2022. Accessed May 17, 2024. https://www.havefunwithhistory.com/black-slave-owners.

History.com. "Stonewall Riots." *History.com*. Updated on June 20, 2024. Accessed October 1, 2024. https://www.history.com/topics/gay-rights/the-stonewall-riots.

Holland, Robert and Don Soifer. "Radical multiculturalism a growing problem in public schools." *The Daily Caller*, September 16, 2010. Accessed July 28. 2024. https://dailycaller.com/2010/09/16/radical-multiculturalism-a-growing-problem-in-public-schools.

Hughes, Dr. Steve. "Cognitive Effects of Montessori on the Brain." *Wake Forest Montessori*. 2012, lecture presented at Wake Forest Montessori, Minnesota, video begins at about 10:50.

Influence Watch. "School of Unity and Liberation (SOUL)." *Influence Watch*. 2024. https://www.influencewatch.org/non-profit/school-of-unity-and-liberation-soul.

"Inmate released early, arrested weeks later for murder." *Law Enforcement Today*. https://www.lawenforcementtoday.com/prison-inmate-released-early-arrested-weeks-later-for-murder.

Innovation Montessori. "Fast Facts." *innovationmontessori.com*. Accessed May 22, 2024.

Izaguirre, Anthony. "Florida Legislature passes 'Don't Say Gay' bill, which Governor Ron DeSantis is expected to sign into law." *Boston Globe*. March 8, 2022. Accessed April 17, 2024. https://www.bostonglobe.com/2022/03/08/nation/florida-legislature-has-passed-dont-say-gay-bill-which-governor-ron-desantis-is-expected-sign-into-law.

Jackson, Deborah. "We Don't Push Children Here." *Montessori International Magazine*. London: 18 Balderton Street, 2003.

Jacob, S. H.. *Your Baby's Mind*. Halbrook, Massachusetts: Bob Adams Inc., 1991.

Jarrow Montessori School. "Diversity Resources." *Jarrow Montessori School*. Accessed May 19, 2024. https://jarrow.org/diversity-resources.

Jones, Alex (@RealAlexJones). "Private Investigator Exposes How Adult Furries Target & Groom Kids In Gaming Communities." *X.com*. August 9, 2024. https://x.com/RealAlexJones/status/1822037456176259237.

Jones, Emily. "Scholar Calls Pedophilia 'An Unchangeable Sexual Orientation' that Should Be Accepted by Society." *CBN*. July 21, 2018. Accessed July 28, 2024. https://www1.cbn.com/cbnnews/health/2018/july/scholar-says-pedophilia-is-an-unchangeable-sexual-orientation-and-should-be-accepted-by-society.

Kaczynki, Andy (@KFILE). "At an event last week, the GOP candidate for governor of Minnesota there are, 'litter boxes in some of the school districts so kids can pee in them, because they identify as a furry…' It's a persistent and bizarre Internet hoax." *X.com*. October 3, 2022.

https://x.com/KFILE/status/1576983730492567552.

Kalleres, Dan. "A Montessori Educator Reflects on the Work of Antiracism Expert and The Montessori Event Keynote Speaker, Ibram X. Kendi." *AMS* (blog). February 01, 2023. Accessed April 28, 2024. https://amshq.org/Blog/2023-02-01-Antiracism-Expert-and-The-Montessori-Event-Keynote-Speaker-Dr-Ibram-X-Kendi.

Keenan, Harper. "Drag Pedagogy: The playful practice of queer imagination in early childhood." *Curriculum Inquiry* 50, no. 5 (2020). Accessed September 30, 2024. https://www.tandfonline.com/doi/full/10.1080/03626784.2020.1864621.

Kincheloe, J. L.. *Critical Pedagogy Primer*. Peter Lang Inc., International Academic Publishers, 2008.

Kohn, Alphie. *Punished by Rewards*. New York: Houghton Mifflin Co.,1993.

Kramer, Rita. *Maria Montessori, A Biography*. New York: Capricorn Books, 1977.

Kulikow, V.. "The Most Frequently Challenged Books and Why." *AMS* (blog). July 26, 2023. Accessed June 8, 2024. https://amshq.org/Blog/2023-07-26-Banned-Books-The-Most-Frequently-Challenged-Books-and-Why.

Kulikow, V.. "Pride Month Reads: LGBTQIA+ Stories for Children and Teens." *AMS*. June 5, 2023. Accessed July 29, 2024. https://amshq.org/Blog/2023-06-05-Pride-Month-Reads-LGBTQIA-Stories-for-Children-and-Teens.

Kumashiro, K. K.. "Against repetition: Addressing resistance to anti-oppressive change in the practices of learning, teaching, supervising, and researching." *Harvard Educational Review* 72, no. 1 (2002).

Kumashiro, Kevin. *Troubling Education: "Queer" Activism and Anti-Oppressive Pedagogy*. London: Routledge, 2002.

Lake Harriet Montessori School. "Lake Harriet Montessori School." *Lake Harriet Montessori School*. Accessed May 5, 2024. https://www.lhms.org.

Lancer, Darlene. "Exploring Autonomy, Locus of Control, and Self-Efficacy." *PsychCentral*. May 17, 2016. https://psychcentral.com/lib/co-dependency-put-the-i-in-independence#1

Lansing, Logan. *The Queering of the American Child*. New Discourses, 2024. Kindle.

Lavietes, Matt. "Florida Gov. Ron DeSantis signals support for 'Don't

Say Gay' bill: The bill, which would bar the 'discussion of sexual orientation or gender identity' in primary schools, passed the Florida Senate Education Committee on Tuesday." Out Politics and Policy. *NBC News.* February 8, 2022. https://www.nbcnews.com/nbc-out/out-politics-and-policy/florida-gov-ron-desantis-signals-support-dont-say-gay-bill-rcna15326.

Leitch, Kathy. "Standing Together…Our Role in Ending Systemic and Internal Racism." *The Montessori Foundation.* June 30, 2020. https://www.montessori.org/standing-together-our-role-in-ending-systemic-and-internal-racism.

Lenin, Vladmir. "The tasks of the youth leagues: Speech delivered at the third all-Russia Congress of the Russian Young Communist League." Transcription of speech given on October 2, 1920. *Marxist Internet Archive.* 1999. Accessed April 16, 2024. https://www.marxists.org/archive/lenin/works/1920/oct/02.htm.

LeShan, Eda J. *The Conspiracy Against Childhood.* New York: Atheneum, 1968.

Lexington Montessori School, Lexington, Massachusetts. "Lexington Montessori School." *Lexington Montessori School.* Accessed September 30, 2024. https://www.lexmontessori.org/student-experience/social-justice.

Libs of TikTok (@libsoftiktok). "BREAKING: Photos have surfaced of "furries" in Nebo School District in Utah. The media and a spokesperson for the school are claiming it's not happening." *X.com.* April 17, 2024. https://x.com/libsoftiktok/status/1781161371465560447.

Libs of TikTok (@libsoftiktok). "The media is going all out to cover up for the furries. There's video & photo evidence, a spokesperson for the school admits students dress up as furries, and students themselves are on camera saying this happening yet the media and the Left (but I repeat myself) are still trying to deny this is happening. Unbelievable." *X.com.* April 18, 2024. https://x.com/libsoftiktok/status/1781156432836243941.

Libs of TikTok (@libsoftiktok). "Rep. Charise Davids (D-KS) attended and promoted an "all ages family friendly" pride event featuring an adult in b*nd*ge gear, furries, and d*ag queens performing s*xual themed dances for children who handed them cash tips." *X.com.* June 24, 2024. https://x.com/libsoftiktok/status/1805351421304619084.

Lillard, Paula Polk. *Montessori: A Modern Approach.* New York: Schocken

Books, 1972.

Lind, William. "Chapter VI Further Readings on the Frankfurt School." *Commons.wikimannia.org*. Accessed April 28, 2024. https://commons.wikimannia.org/images/William_S_Lind_-_Political_Correctness_-_A_Short_History_of_an_Ideology_-_Part_VI.pdf.

Lindsay, James. *The Marxification of Education*. New Discourses. 2022. Kindle.

Lindsay, James. "Queer Theory." *New Discourses*. April 7, 2020. Accessed April 17, 2024. https://newdiscourses.com/tftw-queer-theory.

Lindsay, James. "Woke: A Culture War Against Europe." *NewDiscourses. Substack.com*. March 29, 2023. Woke Conference, at the European Parliament video. Accessed October 25, 2024. https://newdiscourses.substack.com/p/woke-a-culture-war-against-europe.

Littman, Lisa. "Parent reports of adolescents and young adults perceived to show signs of a rapid onset of gender dysphoria." *Plos/One* 14, no. 3 (August 2018). Accessed October 1, 2024. https://journals.plos.org/plosone/article?id=10.1371/journal.pone.0202330.

Livingston, Alexander. "John Dewey's Experiments in Democratic Socialism." *Jacobin*. January 8, 2018. Accessed July 29, 2024. https://jacobin.com/2018/01/john-dewey-democratic-socialism-liberalism.

Locke, Edwin A.. *The Illusion of Determinism, Why Free Will is Real and Causal*. Maryland: Edwin A. Locke, 2017.

Mad Mom. June 28, 2022 (6:14 pm). New Discourse. "Groomer Schools 4: Drag Queen Story Hour." *New Discourses Podcast*. June 27, 2022. Accessed May 20, 2024. https://newdiscourses.com/2022/06/groomer-schools-4-drag-queen-story-hour/#comment-49471.

Marx, Karl and Friedrich Engels. "Manifesto of the Communist Party." *Internet Archive*. 1848. Accessed May 13, 2024. https://archive.org/details/ComManifesto/mode/2up.

Mathnerd, Holly. "The Queering of the American Child: a review of James Lindsay's new book." *Holly's Substack* (blog). February 16, 2024. Accessed April 17, 2024. https://hollymathnerd.substack.com/p/the-queering-of-the-american-child.

Matthews, Timothy. "The Frankfurt School: Conspiracy to Corrupt." *Catholic Insight*. March 2009. http://www.judeochristianamerica.org/ConsReading/The-Frankfurt-School-Timothy-Matthews.pdf

Matthews, Timothy. "Frankfurt School." *World Book Encyclopedia*. https://www.newworldencyclopedia.org/entry/Frankfurt_school.

Merriam-Webster Dictionary. "time-out." *Merriam-Webster Dictionary.* Accessed July 28, 2024. https://www.merriam-webster.com/dictionary/time-out.

Montessori Country School. "Conflict Resolution Models used at Montessori Country School." *Montessori Country School.* Accessed May 22, 2024. https://montessoricountryschool.org/wordpress/wp-content/uploads/2020/02/Conflict-Resolution-at-MCS.pdf.

Montessori for Social Justice. "2023 MSJ Conference: Imagining Liberation…Honoring our Humanity, June 22-25, 2023." *Montessori for Social Justice.* 2023. Accessed May 19, 2024. https://www.montessoriforsocialjustice.org/conference.

Montessori for Social Justice. *Montessori for Social Justice.* Accessed May 20, 2024. https://montessoriforsocialjustice.org.

Montessori, Maria. *The 1946 London Lectures.* vol. 17. The Netherlands: Montessori-Pierson Publishing Company, 1946.

Montessori, Maria. *The Absorbent Mind.* Clio Montessori Press, 1994.

Montessori, Maria. The Absorbent Mind. New York: Dell Publishing, 1967.

Montessori, Maria. The Absorbent Mind. Oxford: Clio Press, 1988.

Montessori, Maria. *The Advanced Montessori Method.* New York: Frederick A. Stokes Company, 1917.

Montessori, Maria. *Advanced Montessori Method I.* India: Kalakshetra Publications, 1965.

Montessori, Maria. *Citizen of the World.* The Netherlands: Montessori-Pierson Publishing Company, 2019.

Montessori, Maria. *The Discovery of the Child.* India: Kalakshetra Publications, 1966.

Montessori, Maria. Education and Peace. The Netherlands: Montessori-Pierson Publishing Company. Accessed September 29, 2024. https://montessori150.org/maria-montessori/montessori-quotes?field_keywords_target_id=All&body_value=normal+child&publication=All.

Montessori, Maria. *Education For A New World.* Archive.org. 1946. Accessed October 1, 2024. https://archive.org/details/in.ernet.dli.2015.36346/page/n43/mode/2up?q=generation.

Montessori, Maria. *Education For A New World.* California: ABC-CLIO, 1989.

Montessori, Maria. "Foreword" of *The Discovery of the Child.* vol. 2. The Netherlands: Montessori-Pierson Publishing Company.

Montessori, Maria. *The Formation of Man*. The Netherlands: Montessori-Pierson Publishing Company, 2007.

Montessori, Maria. *The Montessori Method*. Fresno, California: Schocken Books, Inc., 1964. https://digital.library.upenn.edu/women/montessori/method/method.html.

Montessori, Maria. *The Montessori Method*. New York: Frederick A. Stokes Company, 1912.

Montessori, Maria. *The Montessori Method*. New York: Schocken Books Inc, translated in 1912.

Montessori, Maria. "Preface" in *Education and Peace*. Washington, DC: Regnery, 1972. https://archive.org/details/educationpeace00mont/page/n17/mode/2up?q=crime.

Montessori, Maria. *The Secret of Childhood*. New York: Ballantine Books, 1966.

Montessori, Maria. *The Secret of Childhood*. New York: Fides Publishers, 1966.

Montessori, Maria. *The Secret of Childhood*. vol. 22. The Netherlands: Montessori-Pierson. Accessed April 18, 2024. https://montessori150.org/maria-montessori/montessori-books/secret-childhood.

Montessori, Maria. *Spontaneous Activity in Education*. Accessed April 18, 2024. http://www.readcentral.com/chapters/Maria-Montessori/Spontaneous-Activity-in-Education/008.

Montessori, Maria. *Spontaneous Activity in Education*. Massachusetts: Robert Bentley, Inc., 1917.

Montessori, Maria. *Spontaneous Activity in Education*. New York: Frederick A. Stokes Co., 1917.

Montessori, Maria. *Spontaneous Activity in Education*. New York: Schocken Books, 1965.

Montessori, Maria. *To Educate the Human Potential*. India: Kalakshetra Publications, 1948.

Montessori, Maria. To Educate the Human Potential. vol. 6. The Netherlands: Montessori-Pierson Publishing, 1948.

Myers, Trevor. "Students walk out of middle school to protest 'furries." *ABC.com*. April 17, 2024. Accessed September 30, 2024. https://www.abc4.com/news/wasatch-front/utah-student-furry-protest.

My School DC. "Lee Montessori PCS – Brookland." My School DC. Accessed May 22, 2024. https://www.myschooldc.org/schools/profile/207.

National Center for Montessori in the Public Sector. "A Home for Public Montessori: We sustain Montessori in the public sector through a community network, teacher training, school support, and field-tested tools." *National Center for Montessori in the Public Sector*. 2024. https://www.public-montessori.org.

National Center for Montessori in the Public Sector. "Equity." *National Center for Montessori in the Public Sector*. 2024. Accessed July 30, 2024. https://www.public-montessori.org/about-us/#equity.

Neill, A. S.. *Summerhill*. New York: Hart Publishing, 1960.

Nelsen, Jane. *Positive Discipline for Pre-Schoolers*. New York: Crown Publishing Group, 2007.

Nelsen, Jane. *Positive Discipline*. Ballantine Books. New York, 1987.

Newman, Alex. "How John Dewey Used Public 'Education' to Subvert Liberty." *Illinois Family Institute* (originally published in Epoch Times). 2021. Accessed October 25, 2024. https://illinoisfamily.org/education/how-john-dewey-used-public-education-to-subvert-liberty.

NextNewsNetwork. "BREAKING: FBI Seizes Personal Property of Key Trump Ally, Congressman Scott Perry." *rumble* (video). August 10, 2022. https://rumble.com/v1fjxxm-breaking-fbi-seizes-personal-property-of-key-trump-ally-congressman-scott-p.html.

Off Topic Show (@OffTopicShow2). "From Pipes to Litter Boxes: A Tennessee Tale of Plumbing and Furries: In a bizarre twist of events, a plumber from Tennessee recently shared his experience working in a house where the owner's teenage daughter identifies as a cat and insists on using a giant litter box. This peculiar story has sparked a flurry of discussions and debates on social media, with some expressing disbelief and others sharing similar experiences." *X.com*. June 7, 2024. https://x.com/OffTopicShow2/status/1799094817667809527.

Oliver, Mark. "Horrific Facts About Scalping On The American Frontier." *Listverse*. July 16, 2017. https://listverse.com/2017/07/16/top-10-horrific-facts-about-scalping-on-the-american-frontier.

Parker, Richard. "Thinking Sex: Notes for a Radical Theory of the Politics of Sexuality. By Gayle S. Rubin." Chapter 9 in *Culture Society and Sexuality*. London: Routledge, 2006. https://www.taylorfrancis.com/books/edit/10.4324/9780203966105/culture-society-sexuality-peter-aggleton-richard-parker.

Peikoff, Leonard. *Ominous Parallels*. New York: Stein and Day, 1982.

Peikoff, Leonard. "Why Johnny Can't Think." *The Objectivist Forum* 5, no. 6 (December 1984).

Pisaturo, Ronald. *Masculine Power, Feminine Beauty*. Prime Mover Press, 2021.

Queer Montessori. "Facebook Group: queer montessorians." *Facebook*. Accessed May 7, 2024. Queerhttps://www.facebook.com/groups/435993763813006.

Rahman, Khaleda. "CNN Mocked for calling Kenosha riots 'fiery but mostly peaceful protests'." *Newsweek*. August 27, 2020. https://www.newsweek.com/cnn-mocked-calling-kenosha-riots-fiery-mostly-peaceful-protests-1527997#:~:text=CNN%20has%20been%20mocked%20on%20Twitter%20for%20displaying%20a%20chyron.

Raichik, Chaya (@ChayaRaichik10). "Guys there's no evidence of furries in the Utah school except photos, a clip of a "dog" chasing a student, and a school spokesperson admitting that kids come dressed with animal ears. Other than that, it's totally not happening." *X.com*. April 18, 2024. https://x.com/ChayaRaichik10/status/1781158748914098272.

Rand, Ayn. *Atlas Shrugged*. New York: Random House, 1957.

Rand, Ayn. "The Comprachicos" in *The New Left: The Anti-Industrial Revolution*. New York: New American Library, 1971.

Rand, Ayn. *For the New Intellectual*. New York: Random House, 1961.

Rand, Ayn. *Introduction to Objectivist Epistemology*. New York: Penguin Group, 1979.

Rand, Ayn. *The New Left*. New York: Penguin Group, 1975.

Rand, Ayn. *Philosophy Who Needs It*. Indianapolis/New York: Bobbs-Merrill Company, 1982.

Rand, Ayn. "Screen Guide for Americans." *Plain Talk*. November 1947.

Rand, Ayn. *The Virtue of Selfishness*. New York: The New American Library, 1964.

Red-Coral.net. "Berkeley Indigenous Peoples Day: Pow Wow & Indian Market." *red-coral.net*. 2008. Accessed April 17, 2024. https://www.red-coral.net/Pow.html.

Ridpath, John. "This Hallowed Ground." July 1–7, 1992, paper presented at Objectivist conference, Williamsburg, Virginia.

Robles, Christian. "Closing School Climate Gaps at Elm City Montessori School." *Yale College Education Studies Program*. Spring 2023. Accessed May 22, 2024. https://educationstudies.yale.edu/sites/default/files/files/Christian_Robles_FinalCapstone.pdf.

Rohi's Readery. "Collaborations." *Rohi's Readery.* Accessed June 23, 2024. https://www.rohisreadery.com/collaborations.

Rooke, Mary. "'Look At All That Money You Just Made!': Drag Queen Praises Girl Dancing For Cash Tips." *The Daily Caller.* August 3, 2022. Accessed April 17, 2024. https://dailycaller.com/2022/08/03/drag-queen-girl-dancing-cash-tips-libs-tiktok-viral-video.

Rosemond-Hoerr, Elena. "Creating Safe Schools for LGBTQIA+ Students, Staff." *GoogleDocs.* Accessed April 28, 2024. https://docs.google.com/document/d/1-m6VH9BF0R7Bjf3XOUy5mZcheaaci-2KRUUvCzTnf2gc/edit.

Rosemond-Hoerr, Elena. "On-Demand Webinar: Creating Safe Schools for LGBTQIA+ Students, Staff, and Families a webinar series." *Montessori for Social Justice.* Accessed April 28, 2024. https://www.montessoriforsocialjustice.org/conference/webinars.

RT News. "Catch and release: Rioters jailed in St. Louis and New York set free by local prosecutors." *USA News.* June 3, 2020. https://www.rt.com/usa/490697-rioters-looters-released-prosecutors.

Rubin, Gayle. "Chapter 9 Thinking Sex: Notes for a Radical Theory of the Politics of Sexuality." *Culture Society and Sexuality.* 2006. Accessed April 17, 2024. https://bpb-us-e2.wpmucdn.com/sites.middlebury.edu/dist/2/3378/files/2015/01/Rubin-Thinking-Sex.pdf.

Saint Paul Federation of Educators. "Restorative Practices." *SPFE28.org.* Accessed May22, 2024. https://www.spfe28.org/teaching-and-learning/restorative-practices.

Samenow, Stanton. *Before It's Too Late.* New York: Three Rivers Press, 2001.

Savage, Michael (@ASavageNation). "A Child Thinks he is a Furry Animal: California Law Dictates School Must Provide Litterbox for him in Classroom." *X.com.* July 8, 2023. https://x.com/ASavageNation/status/1677770838781874176.

Sherwood, Amelia. "The Anti-Bias & Anti-Racist Administrator Workshop." *AMI/USA.* November 2, 2020. Accessed May 17, 2024. https://amiusa.org/event/the-anti-bias-anti-racist-administrator.

Sinclair, Lilith Sinclair (@LaughAtLibs). "Black Lives Matter leader Lilith Sinclair says she's "organizing for the abolition of not just the militarized police state but also the United States as we know it." *X.com.* July 17, 2020. https://twitter.com/LaughAtLibs/status/1284254888067600386.

Standing, E. M.. *Maria Montessori: Her Life and Work*. New York: New American Library, 1957.

Standing, E. M.. *The Montessori Method: A Revolution in Education*. Fresno, California: Academy Library Guild, 1962.

Steensma, Thomas D., Jenifer K McGuire, Baudewijntje P.C. Kreukels, Anneke J. Beekman, and Peggy T. Cohen-Kettenis. "Factors Associated With Desistence and Persistence of Childhood Gender Dysphoria: A Quantitative Follow-Up Study." *Journal of the American Academy of Child & Adolescent Psychiatry* 52, no. 6 (June 2013). Accessed May 5, 2024. https://www.transgendertrend.com/wp-content/uploads/2017/10/Steensma-2013_desistance-rates.pdf.

"St. Louis couple facing charges for waving guns at protesters, defend show of weapons, argue Democrats would bring 'crime, lawlessness' to the suburbs in RNC speech." *Baltimore Sun*. August 25, 2020. https://www.baltimoresun.com/news/nation-world/ct-rnc-st-louis-couple-mark-patricia-mccloskey-20200824-ql3vrmsbwzcadjkwse6reel2ca-story.html.

St. Pierre, Kat. "Top 5 Powerful ABAR Podcasts." *AMS* (blog). January 18, 2022. Accessed May 19, 2024. https://amshq.org/Blog/2022_01_15-Top-5-Powerful-ABAR-Podcasts.

Sullivan, Sharon. "'They Are Putting Litter Boxes in Schools for People Who Identify As Cats,' Says Boebert. 'Not True,' Responds Durango School *District." Colorado Times Recorder*. October 4, 2022. https://coloradotimesrecorder.com/2022/10/they-are-putting-litter-boxes-in-schools-for-people-who-identify-as-cats-says-boebert-not-true-responds-durango-school-district/49272.

Taylor, Paul. A Respect for Nature: A Theory of Environmental Ethics. Princeton University Press, 1986.

Tometi, Ayo. "Biography." *Ayo Tometi*. 2024. Accessed September 23, 2024. https://ayotometi.org/biography.

Villa La Pietra, NYU, Florence. "Everything Within the State, Nothing Against the State, Nothing Outside the State: Toward the History of Everyday Life in Fascist Italy." *Villa La Pietra*. November 3, 2015. Accessed April 17, 2024. https://lapietra.nyu.edu/event/everything-within-the-state-nothing-against-the-state-nothing-outside-the-state-toward-the-history-of-everyday-life-in-fascist-italy.

Walsh, David. *No: Why Kids—of All Ages—Need to Hear It and How Parents Can Say It*. New York: Simon and Schuster, 2007.

Walsh, David. *WHY Do They Act That Way?: A Survival Guide to the Adolescent Brain for You and Your Teen*. New York: Free Press, 2005.

Walter, Scott. "The Founders of Black Lives Matter." *Capital Research*. April 5, 2021. Accessed September 24, 2024. https://capitalresearch.org/article/the-founders-of-black-lives-matter.

WebArchive.org. "Our Co-founders." *Black Lives Matter*. https://web.archive.org/web/20190328020756/https://blacklivesmatter.com/about/our-co-founders.

White, Heather. "The Montessorians of Color Affinity Group: A Safe Space for BIPOC." *AMS*. February 06, 2023. Accessed July 29, 2024. https://amshq.org/Blog/2023-02-06-Montessorians-of-Color-A-Safe-Space-for-BIPOC.

Wiggins, Christopher. "The queerest education in America: How LGBTQ+ kids thrive at this Indiana school." *The Advocate*. May 13, 2024. Accessed May 15, 2024. https://www.advocate.com/news/queerest-education-river-montessori-high-school.

Wikipedia. "Marx's theory of human nature." *Wikipedia*. December 2017. Accessed September 30, 2024. https://en.wikipedia.org/wiki/Marx%27s_theory_of_human_nature.

Wikipedia. "Pragmatic theory of truth. *Wikipedia*. Accessed on April 17, 2024. https://en.wikipedia.org/wiki/Pragmatic_theory_of_truth.

Wikipedia. "Stuart Hall (cultural theorist)." *Wikipedia*. 2024. Accessed September 24, 2024. https://en.wikipedia.org/wiki/Stuart_Hall_(cultural_theorist).

Wikipedia. "Trail of Tears." *Wikipedia*. October 16, 2024. https://en.wikipedia.org/wiki/Trail_of_Tears.

Wikramaratne, Lena. "AMI Montessori Training Course." Palo Alto, California, 1972-1973.

Wise, Valaida (Val) L. and Wendy Shenk-Evans. "Critical Race Theory: Talking Through the Confusion." *American Montessori Society*. August 19, 2021. Accessed April 22, 2024. https://amshq.org/Educators/Community/Announcements/All-Announcements/2021/2021-08-05-Critical-Race-Theory-Talking-Through-the-Confusion.

Wolf, Anthony. *Get Out of My Life, But First Could You Drive Me & Cheryl to the Mall: A Parent's Guide to the New Teenager*. New York: Farrar, Straus and Giroux, 2002.

"Woman savagely beaten in NYC subway station describes the pain, trauma." *ABC News*. September 28, 2022. https://abc7chicago.

com/woman-beaten-in-subway-station-waheed-foster-nyc-attack-assault/12277018.

Wood, Paul. *How to Get Your Children to Do What You Want Them To Do*. Pasadena, California: Cassette Works, 1977, audio cassette.

Young, Joshua. "Norway Ethics professor calls for normalization of pedophilia." *The Post Millennial*. June 11, 2022. Accessed July 28, 2024. https://thepostmillennial.com/norway-ethics-professor-calls-for-normalization-of-pedophilia.

Zimmerman, Sarah Cole. "Self-esteem." February 20, 1983, paper presented at workshop, Berkeley, California.

About the Author

Charlotte Cushman is a Montessori educator. She taught at Minnesota Renaissance School, which she owned with her husband, Dan Van Bogart.

She graduated from Lewis and Clark College, Portland, Oregon in 1972 with a B.S. Degree in Elementary Education. While attending college, she went on an overseas program to Japan where she did an independent study project, "Child Discipline in Japan." Immediately after graduation, she took her AMI Montessori training at the Montessori Training Center, Palo Alto, California from Lena Wikramaratne, a colleague and friend of Maria Montessori.

After that, she worked as an assistant teacher at Golden Montessori, Portland, Oregon, moved back to the Midwest and worked as the head teacher at Sunrise Montessori in Anoka, Minnesota. In 1985, she and her best friend, Carol Landkamer, started their own school, Independence Montessori. When Carol retired, Charlotte joined her husband's school, Minnesota Renaissance School, which he had started a few years prior.

She has authored *Montessori: Why It Matters for Your Child's Success and Happiness*, *Your Life Belongs to You* (a children's book about the founding of the United States), and *Effective Discipline the Montessori Way*. She has written numerous articles about child development and has been published in periodicals such as "Montessori Life," "The Montessori Courier," "Public School Montessorian," "Minnesota Parent," "American Thinker," "Capitalism Magazine," and the newsletter for Putting People First. She has delivered presentations on child development, discipline, and the Montessori philosophy and method to community groups, parent groups, Montessori teachers, and schools, Montessori conferences, and the Ayn Rand Institute.

Charlotte takes the development of the child seriously. She is completely devoted to the idea that education, rather than merely presenting knowledge, is needed to develop the child's reasoning mind through reality, order, and logic.

She is a parent and grandparent and enjoys spending time with her family. She also enjoys writing, sewing, quilting, reading, knitting, music, genealogy, talk radio, doll collecting, psychology, and discussing ideas.

www.ingramcontent.com/pod-product-compliance
Lightning Source LLC
Chambersburg PA
CBHW020500030426
42337CB00011B/175